D1093924

In the Name of Allah,
the All-Compassionate, All-Merciful

Title: *MUḤARRAMĀT* — Forbidden matters in Islam some people take lightly

Author: Muhammad Ṣāliḥ al-Munajjid

English Edition 1 (1999)

English Edition 2 (2004)

Layout: IIPH, Riyadh, Saudi Arabia

Filming & Cover Designing: Samo Press Group

Revised Edition Two

Muḥarramāt

Forbidden Matters In Islam Some People Take Lightly

محرَّمات استهان بها الناس

by

Muhammad Ṣāliḥ al-Munajjid

International Islamic Publishing House

© International Islamic Publishing House, 2004
King Fahd National Library Cataloging-in-Publication Data

Al-Munajjid, Muhammad ibn Ṣāliḥ
Muḥarramāt: Forbidden matters some people take lightly .-
Riyadh, 2004

...p ; 20 cm

1- Lawful and unlawful 2- Prohibition and permission
I- Title

ISBN: 9960-672-18-2

253.99 dc 2901/21

Legal Deposit no. **2901/21**
ISBN Soft Cover: **9960-672-18-2**

All rights reserved. No part of this book may be reproduced or transmitted in any form or by any means, electronic or mechanical, including photocopying, recording, or by any information storage and retrieval system, without written permission from the Publisher.

International Islamic Publishing House (IIPH)
P.O.Box 55195 Riyadh 11534, Saudi Arabia
Tel: 966 1 4650818 – 4647213 – Fax: 4633489
E-Mail: iiph@iiph.com.sa – www.iiph.com.sa

---

*Please take part in this noble work by conveying your comments to **IIPH through e-mail, fax or postal-mail address.***

List of Contents

Transliteration Chart

أ	a
آ ـ ى	ā
ب	b
ت	t
ة	h or t (when followed by another Arabic word)
ث	th
ج	j
ح	ḥ
خ	kh
د	d
ذ	dh
ر	r
ز	z
س	s
ش	sh
ص	ṣ
ض	ḍ
ط	ṭ

ظ	dh / ẓ
ع	‘
غ	gh
ف	f
ق	q
ك	k
ل	l
م	m
ن	n
هـ – ه – ـه	h
و	w
و (as a long vowel)	oo
ي	y
ي (as a long vowel)	ee
ء	’ (Omitted in initial position)

َ	Fatḥah	a
ِ	Kasrah	i
ُ	Ḍammah	u
ّ	Shaddah	Double letter
ْ	Sukoon	Absence of vowel

Publisher's Note

Allah (ﷻ) (the Exalted) has explained in the Qur'an, and the Prophet (ﷺ) (Blessings and Peace be upon him) explained in the *Sunnah* the obligations which we should not ignore; He (ﷻ) has also showed us all the evil deeds which no one is allowed to commit. Many Muslims know these obligations and prohibitions in general. And Allah has set for them limits that should not be transgressed. Knowledge is the key to avoiding evil acts for which "ignorance" is never an excuse to commit them. Some Muslims who follow their desires and are weak at heart feel uneasy whenever these *Muḥarramāt* (Forbidden Matters) are mentioned, whereas those who are pious take every opportunity to improve themselves in the right path.

Sheikh al-Munajjid in this book, which is similar to *Manhiyyāt*, has scholarly enumerated and dealt with the prohibitions that no Muslim is allowed to commit.

This is the revised and improved edition of this valuable work. I pray to Allah to grant the readers every benefit and reward the author, translator and all those associated with its publication, *Āmeen*.

Muhammad 'Abdul-Muḥsin Al Tuwaijri

International Islamic Publishing House
Riyadh, Saudi Arabia, 1425 AH / 2004 CE

Introduction

Praise be to Allah; we praise Him and seek His help and forgiveness. We seek refuge with Allah (ﷻ) from the evil of our own souls and from our evil deeds. Whomever Allah guides will never be led astray; and whomever Allah leaves astray, no one will guide. I bear witness that there is no true god but Allah Alone, with no partners or associates, and I bear witness that Muhammad (ﷺ) is His Slave and Messenger.

Allah, be He glorified and exalted, has laid down obligations which we are not permitted to ignore, and has set limits which we are not permitted to transgress, and has set out prohibitions which we are not allowed to violate. The Prophet (ﷺ) said:

> "Whatever Allah has permitted in His Book is allowed, and whatever He has prohibited is forbidden; whatever He has remained silent about is a concession, so accept the concession of Allah, for Allah is never forgetful."[1]

Then he recited the *āyah* (verse):

﴿... وَمَا كَانَ رَبُّكَ نَسِيًّا ﴿٦٤﴾﴾ (سورة مَريَـم: ٦٤)

﴿... and your Lord is never forgetful.﴾

(Qur'an 19: 64)

The things which have been prohibited are the boundaries or limits set by Allah (ﷻ):

[1] Al-Ḥākim, 2/375; classified as *ḥasan* by al-Albāni in *Ghāyat al-Marām*, p. 14.

﴿... وَمَن يَتَعَدَّ حُدُودَ ٱللَّهِ فَقَدْ ظَلَمَ نَفْسَهُۥ ... ﴿١﴾﴾

(سورة الطّلَاق: ١)

﴾... And whosoever transgresses the set limits of Allah, then indeed he has wronged himself...﴿

(Qur'an 65: 1)

Allah has issued a threat to the one who transgresses His set limits and violates His prohibitions, as He (ﷻ) says:

﴿وَمَن يَعْصِ ٱللَّهَ وَرَسُولَهُۥ وَيَتَعَدَّ حُدُودَهُۥ يُدْخِلْهُ نَارًا خَٰلِدًا فِيهَا وَلَهُۥ عَذَابٌ مُّهِينٌ ﴿١٤﴾﴾

(سورة النّسَاء: ١٤)

﴾And whosoever disobeys Allah and His Messenger [Muhammad], and transgresses His limits, He will cast him into Fire, to abide therein; and he shall have a disgraceful torment.﴿ *(Qur'an 4: 14)*

Avoiding that which has been forbidden is a duty, because the Prophet (ﷺ) said:

> "Whatever you have been prohibited to do, avoid it; and whatever you have been commanded to do, do as much of it as you can."[2]

It is well-known that some of those who follow their desires, who are weak at heart and have little knowledge, become irritated when they hear lists of prohibitions. They grumble and mutter, "Everything is *ḥarām* (unlawful), you haven't left us anything that is not forbidden! You make our lives boring and

---

[2] Muslim, *Kitāb al-faḍā'il*, hadith no. 130, 'Abdul-Bāqi edition.

miserable. You don't talk about anything but what is *ḥarām*, while religion is supposed to be easy, not strict, and Allah (ﷻ) is Forgiving and Merciful." In response to such remarks, we say:

Allah, be He glorified, rules as He wills and there is none to put back His judgement. He is All-Wise and All-Aware, and He allows whatever He wills and forbids whatever He wills, be He glorified. One of the basic principles of our being His slaves is that we should accept whatever He decrees and submit fully to it. His rulings stem from His knowledge, wisdom and justice, and are not the matter of frivolity or foolish whims, as He (ﷻ) says:

﴿وَتَمَّتْ كَلِمَتُ رَبِّكَ صِدْقًا وَعَدْلًا ۚ لَا مُبَدِّلَ لِكَلِمَٰتِهِۦ ۚ وَهُوَ ٱلسَّمِيعُ ٱلْعَلِيمُ ﴿١١٥﴾﴾ (سورة الأنعام: ١١٥)

﴿And the Word of your Lord has been fulfilled in truth and in justice. None can change His Words. And He is the All-Hearer, the All-Knower.﴾

(Qur'an 6: 115)

Allah has explained to us the governing principle behind the allowing and prohibiting of various things.

﴿... وَيُحِلُّ لَهُمُ ٱلطَّيِّبَٰتِ وَيُحَرِّمُ عَلَيْهِمُ ٱلْخَبَٰٓئِثَ ... ﴿١٥٧﴾﴾ (سورة الأعراف: ١٥٧)

﴿... he allows them as lawful (*aṭ-Ṭayyibāt*) [i.e., all good and lawful as regards things, deeds, beliefs, persons, foods, etc.], and prohibits them as unlawful (*al-Khabā'ith*) [i.e. all evil and unlawful as regards things, deeds, beliefs, persons, foods, etc.],...﴾

(Qur'an 7: 157)

So what is good and pure is *ḥalāl* (lawful), and what is evil and unclean is *ḥarām*.

The right to determine what is *ḥalāl* and what is *ḥarām* belongs to Allah Alone. Whoever claims this right or affirms it for someone else is a *kāfir* (disbeliever) whose extreme *kufr* (disbelief) places him beyond the pale of Islam, as Allah (ﷻ) says:

﴿أَمْ لَهُمْ شُرَكَٰٓؤُاْ شَرَعُواْ لَهُم مِّنَ ٱلدِّينِ مَا لَمْ يَأْذَنۢ بِهِ ٱللَّهُ ... ﴿٢١﴾﴾ (سورة الشّورىٰ: ٢١)

﴿Or have they partners [false gods] who have instituted for them a religion which Allah has not allowed?...﴾ *(Qur'an 42: 21)*

Furthermore, no one is allowed to speak about matters of *ḥalāl* and *ḥarām* except those who have knowledge of the Qur'an and *Sunnah*. Allah (ﷻ) has issued a stern warning to those who speak about *ḥalāl* and *ḥarām* with no knowledge.

﴿وَلَا تَقُولُواْ لِمَا تَصِفُ أَلْسِنَتُكُمُ ٱلْكَذِبَ هَٰذَا حَلَٰلٌ وَهَٰذَا حَرَامٌ لِّتَفْتَرُواْ عَلَى ٱللَّهِ ٱلْكَذِبَ ... ﴿١١٦﴾﴾ (سورة النّحل: ١١٦)

﴿And say not concerning that which your tongues put forth falsely: 'This is lawful and this is forbidden,' so as to invent lies against Allah...﴾ *(Qur'an 16: 116)*

Things which are definitively forbidden have been clearly stated in the Qur'an and *Sunnah*, as Allah (ﷻ) says:

﴿۞ قُلْ تَعَالَوْا۟ أَتْلُ مَا حَرَّمَ رَبُّكُمْ عَلَيْكُمْ ۖ أَلَّا تُشْرِكُوا۟
بِهِۦ شَيْـًٔا ۖ وَبِٱلْوَٰلِدَيْنِ إِحْسَٰنًا ۖ وَلَا تَقْتُلُوٓا۟ أَوْلَٰدَكُم مِّنْ إِمْلَٰقٍ ۖ
... ﴿١٥١﴾﴾

(سورة الأنعام: ١٥١)

﴿Say [O' Muhammad]: 'Come, I will recite what your Lord has prohibited you from: Join not anything in worship with Him; be good and dutiful to your parents; kill not your children because of poverty...﴾

(Qur'an 6: 151)

The *Sunnah* also mentions many prohibitions; for example, the Prophet (ﷺ) said:

> "Allah has forbidden the sale of wine (intoxicants), dead meat, pork and idols."[3]
>
> "Whatever Allah has forbidden, its price is also forbidden."[4]

Some texts mention specific types or groups of prohibitions, such as when Allah (سبحانه وتعالى) forbids certain types of food:

﴿حُرِّمَتْ عَلَيْكُمُ ٱلْمَيْتَةُ وَٱلدَّمُ وَلَحْمُ ٱلْخِنزِيرِ وَمَآ أُهِلَّ لِغَيْرِ ٱللَّهِ بِهِۦ
وَٱلْمُنْخَنِقَةُ وَٱلْمَوْقُوذَةُ وَٱلْمُتَرَدِّيَةُ وَٱلنَّطِيحَةُ وَمَآ أَكَلَ ٱلسَّبُعُ إِلَّا مَا
ذَكَّيْتُمْ وَمَا ذُبِحَ عَلَى ٱلنُّصُبِ وَأَن تَسْتَقْسِمُوا۟ بِٱلْأَزْلَٰمِ ... ﴿٣﴾﴾

(سورة المائدة: ٣)

---

[3] Abu Dāwood, hadith no. 3486; see also *Ṣaḥeeḥ Abu Dāwood*, hadith no. 977.

[4] Ad-Dāraquṭni, 3/7; it is a *ṣaḥeeḥ* hadith.

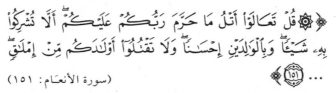

﴿Forbidden to you [for food] are: *al-Mayitah* [the dead animals — cattle — beast not slaughtered], blood, the flesh of swine, and that on which Allah's Name has not been mentioned while slaughtering, [meat of that which has been slaughtered as a sacrifice for other than Allah, or has been slaughtered for idols], and that which has been killed by strangling, or by a violent blow, or by a headlong fall, or by the goring of horns — and that which has been [partly] eaten by a wild animal — unless you are able to slaughter it [before its death] — and that which is sacrificed [slaughtered] on *an-Nuṣub* [stone altars]. Forbidden also is to use arrows seeking luck or decision;...﴾ *(Qur'an 5: 3)*

Allah has also mentioned that which is forbidden with regard to marriage, as He (ﷻ) says:

﴿حُرِّمَتْ عَلَيْكُمْ أُمَّهَٰتُكُمْ وَبَنَاتُكُمْ وَأَخَوَٰتُكُمْ وَعَمَّٰتُكُمْ وَخَٰلَٰتُكُمْ وَبَنَاتُ ٱلْأَخِ وَبَنَاتُ ٱلْأُخْتِ وَأُمَّهَٰتُكُمُ ٱلَّٰتِىٓ أَرْضَعْنَكُمْ وَأَخَوَٰتُكُم مِّنَ ٱلرَّضَٰعَةِ وَأُمَّهَٰتُ نِسَآئِكُمْ ... ﴿٢٣﴾﴾

(سورة النِّسَاء: ٢٣)

﴿Forbidden to you [for marriage] are: your mothers, your daughters, your sisters, your father's sisters, your mother's sisters, your brother's daughters, your sister's daughters, your foster mothers who gave you suck, your foster milk-suckling sisters, your wives' mothers,...﴾ *(Qur'an 4: 23)*

Allah (ﷻ) also mentions what kind of earnings are forbidden, as He says:

﴿... وَأَحَلَّ ٱللَّهُ ٱلْبَيْعَ وَحَرَّمَ ٱلرِّبَوٰاْ ... ﴿٢٧٥﴾﴾

(سورة البقرة: ٢٧٥)

﴾... Allah has permitted trading and forbidden *ribā* [usury]...﴿ *(Qur'an 2: 275)*

Allah, Who is All-Merciful towards His slaves, has permitted innumerable good things, of many kinds. He has not described the permitted things in detail because they are so many; in contrast, He has described the prohibitions in detail because they are limited, so that we will be aware of them and can avoid them. Allah (ﷻ) says:

﴿... فَصَّلَ لَكُم مَّا حَرَّمَ عَلَيْكُمْ إِلَّا مَا ٱضْطُرِرْتُمْ إِلَيْهِ ... ﴿١١٩﴾﴾

(سورة الأنعام: ١١٩)

﴾... He has explained to you in detail what is forbidden to you, except under compulsion of necessity?...﴿ *(Qur'an 6: 119)*

But what is *ḥalāl* is permitted as a general principle, as long as it is good and pure:

﴿يَٰٓأَيُّهَا ٱلنَّاسُ كُلُواْ مِمَّا فِى ٱلْأَرْضِ حَلَٰلًا طَيِّبًا ... ﴿١٦٨﴾﴾

(سورة البقرة: ١٦٨)

﴾O' mankind! Eat of that which is lawful and good on the earth...﴿ *(Qur'an 2: 168)*

It is a part of His Mercy that He has made all things *ḥalāl* in principle, except where there is proof (*daleel*) that they are *ḥarām* (forbidden). This is part of His generosity and bounty towards His slaves, for which we must obey Him, and give praise and thanks to Him.

When some people hear a detailed list of the things that are *ḥarām*, they become alarmed about the rules of *Sharee'ah* (Islamic Law). This is due to their weak faith and poor understanding of Islam. One cannot help wondering whether these people really want to be given a list of every type of thing that is *ḥalāl*, so that they can be convinced that Islam is easy! Do they want us to enumerate every type of good thing so that they can rest assured that Islam will not make their lives dreary?

Do they want to be told that the meat of camels, cattle, sheep, rabbits, deer, goats, chickens, pigeons, ducks, geese and ostriches over which the name of Allah has been mentioned, and fish and locusts are all *ḥalāl*?

That vegetables, herbs, fruits and edible seeds are *ḥalāl*?

That water, milk, honey, oil and vinegar are *ḥalāl*?

That salt, seasonings and spices are *ḥalāl*?

That using wood, iron, sand, stones, plastic, glass and rubber is *ḥalāl*?

That travelling via riding-beasts, cars, trains, ships and airplanes is *ḥalāl*?

That using air-conditioners, fridges, washing-machines, tumble-dryers, mills, dough-mixers, meat-grinders, juicers, medical instruments, engineering tools, calculators, microscopes, telescopes, machinery for extracting water, oil and minerals, filters for purifying water, printing presses and so on is *ḥalāl*?

That wearing cotton, linen, wool, camel hair, fur, permitted leathers, nylon and polyester is *ḥalāl*?

That, in principle, marriage, buying, selling, sponsorship, bills of exchange, renting, professions and trades such as carpentry, metalworking, repairing machines and tending sheep are all *ḥalāl*?

I wonder what would happen if we were to explain all this in detail to them.

﴿... فَمَالِ هَٰٓؤُلَآءِ ٱلْقَوْمِ لَا يَكَادُونَ يَفْقَهُونَ حَدِيثًا ﴿٧٨﴾﴾

(سورة النِّسَاء: ٧٨)

﴿... And what is wrong with these people that they fail to understand any word?﴾ *(Qur'an 4: 78)*

As regards their claim that Islam is easy, this is true, but they are twisting the truth to try and prove something that is false. What is meant by saying that Islam is easy is not that it is in accordance with their desires and opinions, but that it is easy in accordance with what the *Sharee'ah* has brought. There is a gulf of difference between violating prohibitions by making false claims about Islam being easy — although it is easy, beyond any doubt — and availing oneself of legitimate concessions such as being allowed to join or shorten prayers, to break one's fast when travelling, to wipe one's socks when performing *wuḍoo'* (ablution) — for one day and one night for a person who is not travelling, and for three days and three nights in the case of travelling — to perform *tayammum* (dry ablution) when one is afraid to use water, to join two prayers together when one is sick or when it is raining; to look at a non-*maḥram* (marriageable) woman for purposes of marriage, to have the choice, in the case of making expiation for a broken vow, between freeing a slave or feeding or clothing the poor; to eat the meat of dead animals when necessary — and other kinds of concessions allowed by *Sharee'ah*.

In addition to the above, a Muslim should realize that one principle underlies all the prohibitions in Islam: Allah (ﷻ) is testing His slaves by means of these prohibitions, to see what they will do. One of the things that distinguish the people of Paradise from the people of Hell is that the people of Hell indulge in the desires with which the Fire is surrounded, whereas the people of Paradise patiently endure the hardships with which the Garden is surrounded. Were it not for this test, the obedient would not be distinguished from the disobedient. People of faith look at the difficulties involved from the perspective of the reward they will earn by pleasing Allah (ﷻ), so obedience becomes easy for them. The hypocrites, on the other hand, view these difficulties as a matter of pain, suffering and deprivation, so obedience becomes a heavy burden on them.

By foregoing what is prohibited, the obedient person gains much more: whoever forsakes something for the sake of Allah, Allah (ﷻ) will compensate him with something better, and he will enjoy the sweet taste of faith in his heart.

This booklet discusses a number of the prohibitions that have been proven in *Sharee'ah*, based on evidence from the Qur'an and *Sunnah*[5]. These prohibitions include actions which are widely practised among many Muslims. By mentioning them, my intention is to correct and advise people. I ask Allah to guide

---

[5] Some scholars have grouped the prohibitions under headings such as *al-kabā'ir* or major sins. Among the best books on the topic is *Tanbeeh al-ghāfileen 'an A'māl al-jāhileen* by Ibn an-Naḥḥās ad-Dimashqi, may Allah have mercy on him.

me and my Muslim brothers, and to help us to adhere to the limits which He has set and to avoid the things that He has prohibited, and to save us from our evil deeds. And Allah is the Best to guard, and He is the All-Merciful of those who show mercy.

MUḤARRAMĀT — Forbidden matters in Islam some people take lightly

1. *Ash-Shirk* — Associating partners with Allah

This is the most serious of all prohibitions, according to the hadith narrated by Abu Bakrah, who said that the Messenger of Allah (ﷺ) said:

> " 'Shall I not tell you of the most serious of the major sins?' he said it three times. We said, 'Of course, O' Messenger of Allah!' He said, 'Associating anything in worship with Allah...' "[1]

Every other sin may be forgiven by Allah, apart from *ash-shirk*, which requires specific repentance, as Allah (ﷻ) says:

> ﴿إِنَّ ٱللَّهَ لَا يَغْفِرُ أَن يُشْرَكَ بِهِۦ وَيَغْفِرُ مَا دُونَ ذَٰلِكَ لِمَن يَشَآءُ ... ﴿٤٨﴾﴾ (سورة النِّسَاء: ٤٨)

> ﴿Verily, Allah forgives not that partners be set up with Him [in worship], but He forgives what is less than that for whom He wills;...﴾ *(Qur'an 4: 48)*

One of the forms of *ash-shirk*, which is particularly widespread in Muslim countries, is grave-worship.

---

[1] Bukhāri and Muslim; see Bukhāri, hadith no. 2511, al-Baghā edition.

2. Grave-worship

Some people have the belief that dead *awliyā'* (saints) can fulfil their needs or help at times of distress, so they call upon them for aid. Allah (ﷻ) says:

﴿وَقَضَىٰ رَبُّكَ أَلَّا تَعْبُدُوٓا۟ إِلَّآ إِيَّاهُ ... ﴿٢٣﴾﴾

(سورة الإسراء: ٢٣)

﴿And your Lord has decreed that you worship none but Him...﴾ *(Qur'an 17: 23)*

Similarly, they call upon dead Prophets, righteous people and others to intercede for them or to rescue them from some calamity, but Allah (ﷻ) says:

﴿أَمَّن يُجِيبُ ٱلْمُضْطَرَّ إِذَا دَعَاهُ وَيَكْشِفُ ٱلسُّوٓءَ وَيَجْعَلُكُمْ خُلَفَآءَ ٱلْأَرْضِ ۗ أَءِلَـٰهٌ مَّعَ ٱللَّهِ ... ﴿٦٢﴾﴾ (سورة النمل: ٦٢)

﴿Is not He [better than your gods] Who responds to the distressed one, when he calls on Him, and Who removes the evil, and makes you inheritors of the earth? Is there any *ilāh* [god] with Allah?...﴾ *(Qur'an 27: 62)*

Some of them have adopted the habit of mentioning the name of a sheikh or *wali* (saint) when they stand up, or sit down, or stumble, or encounter problems or distress, so they might say 'O' Muhammad!' or 'O' 'Ali!' or 'O' Ḥusayn!' or 'O' Badawi!' or 'O' Jeelāni!' or 'O' Shādhili!' or 'O' Rifā'i!' — or they may call upon al-'Aydaroos or Sayyidah Zaynab or Ibn 'Alwān. Allah says:

﴿إِنَّ ٱلَّذِينَ تَدۡعُونَ مِن دُونِ ٱللَّهِ عِبَادٌ أَمۡثَالُكُمۡۖ ... ﴿١٩٤﴾﴾

(سورة الأعراف: ١٩٤)

﴿Verily, those whom you call upon besides Allah are slaves like you...﴾ *(Qur'an 7: 194)*

Some of those who worship graves walk around them as if in *Ṭawāf* (circumambulation), and acknowledge their corners, or touch them, kiss them, wipe their faces with their dust, prostrate towards them when they see them, or stand before them in fear and humility, praying for whatever they need of healing from some disease, or for a child, or for help with some difficulty. Sometimes they call upon the occupant of the grave, saying, 'O' my master, I have come to you from far away, so do not let me down.' But Allah (ﷻ) says:

﴿وَمَنۡ أَضَلُّ مِمَّن يَدۡعُواْ مِن دُونِ ٱللَّهِ مَن لَّا يَسۡتَجِيبُ لَهُۥٓ إِلَىٰ يَوۡمِ ٱلۡقِيَٰمَةِ وَهُمۡ عَن دُعَآئِهِمۡ غَٰفِلُونَ ﴿٥﴾﴾ (سورة الأحقاف: ٥)

﴿And who is more astray than he who invokes besides Allah those who will not answer him till the Day of Resurrection, and who are [even] unaware of their invocation to them﴾ *(Qur'an 46: 5)*

The Prophet (ﷺ) said:

> "Whoever dies calling on someone else as a rival to Allah will enter Hell."[2]

Some of them shave their heads at the graves, and some have books with titles like *Manāsik Ḥajj* al-Mashāhid (*The Rituals of Pilgrimage to Shrines*), *mashāhid* or shrines referring to graves

---

[2] Bukhāri, See *Fatḥ al-Bāri*, 8/176.

or tombs of *awliyā'* (saints). Some of them believe that the *awliyā'* are running the affairs of the universe and that they have the power to benefit or harm.

Allah (ﷻ) says:

﴿وَإِن يَمْسَسْكَ ٱللَّهُ بِضُرٍّ فَلَا كَاشِفَ لَهُۥٓ إِلَّا هُوَ ۖ وَإِن يُرِدْكَ بِخَيْرٍ فَلَا رَآدَّ لِفَضْلِهِۦ ۚ ... ﴿١٠٧﴾﴾ (سورة يونس: ١٠٧)

﴾And if Allah touches you with hurt, there is none who can remove it but He, and if He intends any good for you, there is none who can repel His Favour...﴿ *(Qur'an 10: 107)*

It is also *shirk* to make a vow to other than Allah (ﷻ), as is done by those who vow to bring candles or lights for the occupants of the graves.

Another manifestation of *ash-shirk al-akbar* (major shirk) is sacrificing to anything other than Allah. Allah (ﷻ) says:

﴿فَصَلِّ لِرَبِّكَ وَٱنْحَرْ ﴿٢﴾﴾ (سورة الكوثر: ٢)

﴾Therefore turn in prayer to your Lord and sacrifice [to Him only].﴿ *(Qur'an 108: 2)*

— i.e., sacrifice to Allah and in the name of Allah. The Prophet (ﷺ) said:

"Allah will curse the one who sacrifices to anything other than Allah."[3]

This sin combines two *ḥarām* deeds: that of sacrificing to anything other than Allah and that of sacrificing in the name of

[3] Muslim, hadith no. 1978, 'Abdul-Bāqi edition.

anything other than Allah, both of which make the meat of the animal slaughtered *ḥarām*. One of the forms of sacrificing to anything other than Allah, which was known during the first *Jāhiliyyah* (pre-Islam period) and is still widespread nowadays, is the practice of 'offering a sacrifice to jinn,' whereby upon buying or constructing a house, or digging a well, people slaughter an animal at its entrance, out of fear of harm from the resident jinn.[4]

Another widespread form of major *shirk* is the sin of allowing what Allah has forbidden and forbidding what Allah has allowed, or believing that anyone has the right to do so except Allah, or referring matters for judgement to *jāhili* (non-Islamic) courts freely and by choice, and believing that this is permissible. Allah (ﷻ) has mentioned this form of major *kufr* (desbelief) in the Qur'an:

﴿ٱتَّخَذُوٓا۟ أَحْبَارَهُمْ وَرُهْبَـٰنَهُمْ أَرْبَابًا مِّن دُونِ ٱللَّهِ ... ﴿٣١﴾﴾

(سورة التوبة: ٣١)

﴿They [Jews and Christians] took their rabbis and their monks as their lords besides Allah [by obeying them in things which they made lawful or unlawful according to their own desires without being ordered by Allah],...﴾ *(Qur'an 9: 31)*

When 'Adiyy ibn Ḥātim heard the Prophet (ﷺ) recite this *āyah*, he said:

"But they were not worshipping them." The Prophet replied, "Yes, but they permitted things that Allah had forbidden, and the people accepted this, and they

---

[4] See *Tayseer al-'Azeez al-Ḥameed, al-Iftā'* edition, p. 158.

forbade things that Allah had allowed, and the people accepted this too, and this is a form of worshipping them."[5]

Allah (ﷻ) described the *mushrikeen* (polytheists) as:

﴿... وَلَا يُحَرِّمُونَ مَا حَرَّمَ ٱللَّهُ وَرَسُولُهُۥ وَلَا يَدِينُونَ دِينَ ٱلْحَقِّ ... ﴿٢٩﴾﴾ (سورة التوبة: ٢٩)

﴿... [those who] do not forbid that which has been forbidden by Allah and His Messenger and [those who] acknowledge not the religion of Truth [i.e. Islam]...﴾ *(Qur'an 9: 29)*

And Allah (ﷻ) said:

﴿قُلْ أَرَءَيْتُم مَّآ أَنزَلَ ٱللَّهُ لَكُم مِّن رِّزْقٍ فَجَعَلْتُم مِّنْهُ حَرَامًا وَحَلَٰلًا قُلْ ءَآللَّهُ أَذِنَ لَكُمْ أَمْ عَلَى ٱللَّهِ تَفْتَرُونَ ﴿٥٩﴾﴾

(سورة يونس: ٥٩)

﴿Say [O' Muhammad]: 'Did you see what provision Allah has sent down to you! And you have made of it lawful and unlawful?' Say [O' Muhammad]: 'Has Allah permitted you [to do so], or do you invent a lie against Allah?'﴾ *(Qur'an 10: 59)*

Other widespread forms of *shirk* are:

---

[5] Al-Bayhaqi in *as-Sunan al-Kubrā*, 10/116. At-Tirmidhi, hadith no. 3095. Al-Albāni classified it as *ḥasan* in *Ghāyat al-Marām*, p. 19.

3. Magic, fortune-telling and divination

Magic (*aṣ-siḥr*) is an act of *kufr* (disbelief), and one of the seven sins which doom a person to Hell. It causes harm but no benefit. Allah (ﷻ) says of the one who learns it:

﴿... وَيَتَعَلَّمُونَ مَا يَضُرُّهُمْ وَلَا يَنفَعُهُمْ ... ﴿١٠٢﴾﴾

(سورة البَقَرَة: ١٠٢)

﴿... And they learn that which harms them and profits them not...﴾ *(Qur'an 2: 102)*

﴿... وَلَا يُفْلِحُ ٱلسَّاحِرُ حَيْثُ أَتَىٰ ﴿٦٩﴾﴾ (سورة طه: ٦٩)

﴿... and the magician will never be successful, no matter what amount [of skill] he may attain.﴾ *(Qur'an 20: 69)*

The one who deals in magic is a *kāfir* (disbeliever), as Allah (ﷻ) says:

﴿... وَمَا كَفَرَ سُلَيْمَٰنُ وَلَٰكِنَّ ٱلشَّيَٰطِينَ كَفَرُوا۟ يُعَلِّمُونَ ٱلنَّاسَ ٱلسِّحْرَ وَمَآ أُنزِلَ عَلَى ٱلْمَلَكَيْنِ بِبَابِلَ هَٰرُوتَ وَمَٰرُوتَ وَمَا يُعَلِّمَانِ مِنْ أَحَدٍ حَتَّىٰ يَقُولَآ إِنَّمَا نَحْنُ فِتْنَةٌ فَلَا تَكْفُرْ ... ﴿١٠٢﴾﴾

(سورة البَقَرَة: ١٠٢)

﴿...Sulaymān did not disbelieve, but the *Shayāṭeen* [devils] disbelieved, teaching men magic and such things as came down at Babylon to the two angels, Hāroot and Māroot, but neither of these two [angels] taught anyone [such things] till they said, 'We are only for trial, so disbelieve not [by learning this magic from us].'...﴾ *(Qur'an 2: 102)*

The prescribed punishment for the one who practices magic is death, and his income is *ḥarām* and impure. But people who are ignorant wrongdoers and weak in faith go to magicians to help them harm someone or take revenge on someone. Some people commit the sin of going to a magician to ask his help in undoing the magic of someone else, when they should turn to Allah (ﷻ) to help them and heal them by reciting His words, such as the *soorahs* (chapters of the Qur'an) that offer protection (*al-Falaq* and *an-Nās*), and so on.

Fortune-tellers and their ilk are *kuffār* (disbelievers) who disbelieve in Allah (ﷻ), because they claim knowledge of the unseen that no one has knowledge of except Allah. Many of these fortune-tellers take advantage of simple-minded people and take their money. They use many methods such as drawing lines in the sand, throwing sea-shells, reading palms, teacups (or coffee cups), crystal balls and mirrors, and so on. If they get it right one time, they get it wrong ninety-nine times; but ignorant people remember only the one time when these liars get something right. They go to them to find out about the future, whether they will be successful in marriage or business, or to help them find something they have lost, and so on. The ruling concerning the person who visits a fortune-teller is: if he believes what he says, he is a *kāfir* who has left Islam, on the basis of the hadith in which the Prophet (ﷺ) said:

> "Whoever goes to a fortune-teller or a soothsayer and believes in what he says has disbelieved in what was revealed to Muhammad."[6]

---

[6] Aḥmad, 2/429; see also *Ṣaḥeeḥ al-Jāmi'*, hadith no. 5939.

If a person does not believe that they have knowledge of the unseen but he goes [to them] out of curiosity or whatever, he is not a *kāfir*, but his prayers will not be accepted for forty days, as the Prophet (ﷺ) said:

> "Whoever goes to a fortune-teller and asks him about something, his prayers will not be accepted for forty nights."[7]

Even though, it is still obligatory to pray and to repent of this sin.

4. Astrology, or believing that the stars and planets have an influence on people's lives and events

Zayd ibn Khālid al-Juhani reported: "The Messenger of Allah (ﷺ) led us in the morning prayer at al-Ḥudaybiyah after it had rained during the night. When he had finished, he turned around to face the people and said:

> "Do you know what your Lord says?' They said, 'Allah and His Messenger know best.' He said: '(Allah says): This morning one of My slaves became a believer in Me and one became a disbeliever. As for the one who said, 'We have been given rain by the grace and mercy of Allah,' he is a believer in Me and a disbeliever in the stars; as for the one who said, 'We have been given rain by such-and-such a star,' he is a disbeliever in Me and a believer in the stars.'"[8]

---

[7] Muslim, 4/1751.

[8] Bukhāri; see *Fatḥ al-Bāri*, 2/333.

Similarly, the one who reads the horoscopes in newspapers and magazines and believes in what they say about the influence of the stars and planets is a *mushrik* (polytheist), and the one who reads them for entertainment is a sinner, because it is not permitted to entertain oneself by reading things that contain *shirk* (polytheism), because satan will try to lead him to *ash-shirk* through this.

Another form of *ash-shirk* is believing that certain things can bring benefit when the Creator has not made them so. For example, some people believe in amulets and spells, or wearing certain types of pearls or seashells or metal earrings and so on, upon the advice of fortune-tellers or magicians or in accordance with inherited customs. So, they hang them around their own or their children's necks to ward off the evil eye — or so they claim; or they tie them onto their bodies or hang them in their cars and homes, or wear rings with special stones, thinking that these things can relieve or ward off distress. This, without a doubt, is contrary to the idea of relying on Allah (ﷻ), and will only result in making a person even weaker, like seeking medicine in a *ḥarām* way. These amulets obviously contain much *shirk*, such as seeking the help of some jinn and devils, or vague drawings and illegible writing. Some of these liars even write *āyāt* (verses) from the Qur'an, or mix them with words of *shirk*, or write them with impure substances such as menstrual blood. Hanging up these amulets or tying them to one's body is *ḥarām* because the Prophet (ﷺ) said:

"Whoever hangs up an amulet is guilty of *shirk*."[9]

---

[9] Aḥmad, 4/156; see also *Silsilat al-aḥādeeth aṣ-Ṣaḥeeḥah*, hadith no. 492.

If the one who does this believes that these things can cause benefit or harm instead of Allah, he is a *mushrik* who is guilty of major *shirk*. If he believes that they are a means of causing benefit or harm, then he is a *mushrik* who is guilty of minor *shirk*, which includes *shirk* that consists of attributing causes to things other than Allah.

5. Showing off in worship

Among the conditions for any good deed to be acceptable are that it should be free of any kind of showing off and within the framework of the *Sunnah*. The person who performs acts of worship, like praying, in order to be seen by other people is a *mushrik* and his deed is unacceptable. Allah (ﷻ) says:

﴿إِنَّ ٱلْمُنَٰفِقِينَ يُخَٰدِعُونَ ٱللَّهَ وَهُوَ خَٰدِعُهُمْ وَإِذَا قَامُوٓا۟ إِلَى ٱلصَّلَوٰةِ قَامُوا۟ كُسَالَىٰ يُرَآءُونَ ٱلنَّاسَ وَلَا يَذْكُرُونَ ٱللَّهَ إِلَّا قَلِيلًا ١٤٢﴾

(سورة النِّسَاء: ١٤٢)

﴿Verily, the hypocrites [seek to] deceive Allah, but He is their deceiver. And when they stand up for *aṣ-Ṣalāt* [the prayer], they stand lazily to be seen by people and they do not remember Allah but a little.﴾

(Qur'an 4: 142)

Similarly, the person who does a good deed so that news of it will reach other people has also fallen into the sin of *shirk*. The threat of punishment for the one who does this was reported in the hadith narrated by Ibn 'Abbās, may Allah be pleased with him and his father, in which the Prophet (ﷺ) said:

> "Whoever does things to be seen and heard by others, Allah will cause him to be seen and heard as an example to others."[10]

Whoever does any act of worship for the sake of Allah and other people, his deeds will be unacceptable, as is stated in the hadith *Qudsi*:

> "I am so Self-Sufficient that I am in no need of having an associate. Thus, he who does a deed for someone else's sake as well as Mine will have that deed renounced by Me to the one he associated with Me."[11]

It may happen that a person starts to do a deed for the sake of Allah, then the urge to show off comes over him. If he resists that impulse, his deed will still be acceptable, but if he submits willingly to it, then in the opinion of most of the scholars his deed will be unacceptable.

6. Superstitious belief in omens

Superstitious belief in omens is a form of pessimism, as Allah (سبحانه وتعالى) says:

﴿فَإِذَا جَآءَتۡهُمُ ٱلۡحَسَنَةُ قَالُواْ لَنَا هَٰذِهِۦۖ وَإِن تُصِبۡهُمۡ سَيِّئَةٞ يَطَّيَّرُواْ بِمُوسَىٰ وَمَن مَّعَهُۥٓۗ ... ﴿١٣١﴾﴾ (سورة الأعراف: ١٣١)

﴾But whenever good came to them, they said: 'Ours is this.' And if evil afflicted them, they ascribed it to

[10] Muslim, 4/2289.

[11] Muslim, hadith no. 2985.

evil omens connected with Moosa and those with him...﴾ *(Qur'an 7: 131)*

Before Islam, if one of the Arabs wanted to do something like travelling, he would take hold of a bird and release it. If it flew to the right, he would take this as a good omen and proceed with his plans, but if it flew to the left, he would take it as a bad omen and cancel his plans. The Prophet (ﷺ) gave his verdict on this practice when he said:

"*Aṭ-Ṭiyarah* (observing birds for omens) is *shirk.*"[12]

This kind of *ḥarām* belief that goes against *Tawḥeed* (Unity of God) also includes the practice of regarding certain times as inauspicious, such as not holding a wedding in the month of Safar, or regarding the last Wednesday of every month as a day of evil omen and ongoing calamity, or believing that numbers such as thirteen, or certain names, are 'unlucky.' It is also *ḥarām* to believe that handicapped people are bad omens, such as going to open one's store but turning back upon seeing a one-eyed man. All of this is *ḥarām* and is part of the *shirk* for which the Prophet (ﷺ) disowned people. 'Imrān ibn Ḥuṣayn reported that the Prophet (ﷺ) said:

"He is not one of us who observes birds for omens or has someone else do this for him, or who predicts the future or asks someone else to do it for him, (and I think he said) or who practices magic or asks someone else to do it for him."[13]

---

[12] Aḥmad, 1/389; see also *Ṣaḥeeḥ al-Jāmi'*, hadith no. 3955.

[13] Aṭ-Ṭabarāni: *al-Kabeer*, 18/162; see also *Ṣaḥeeḥ al-Jāmi'*, hadith no. 5435.

The expiation required from the person who commits any of these sins is stated in the hadith reported by ‘Abdullah ibn ‘Amr: “The Messenger of Allah (ﷺ) said:

> ‘Whoever was turned away from doing something because of a bad omen is guilty of *ash-shirk.*’ The people asked, ‘O’ Messenger of Allah! What expiation is there for doing that?’ He said, ‘That he should say: ‘O’ Allah! There is no goodness except Your goodness and no omen except your omen and there is no true god but You.’ ”[14]

Pessimism is a part of everyone’s nature, to a greater or lesser extent; the best cure for it is reliance upon Allah (*at-Tawakkul*), as Ibn Mas‘ood (رضي الله عنه) said:

> “There is no one among us (who will not feel pessimistic sometimes), but when we rely on Allah, He makes that feeling go away.”[15]

7. Swearing by something other than Allah

Allah may swear by whatever of His creatures He wills, but His creatures are not permitted to swear by anything other than Allah (سبحانه وتعالى). Many people swear all kinds of oaths by things other than Allah, but swearing by something is like glorifying it, and it is not right to glorify anything or anyone other than Allah. Ibn ‘Umar (رضي الله عنه) reported that the Prophet (ﷺ) said:

---

[14] Aḥmad, 2/220; *Silsilat al-aḥādeeth aṣ-Ṣaḥeeḥah*, hadith no. 1065.

[15] Abu Dāwood, hadith no. 3910; see also *Silsilat al-aḥādeeth aṣ-Ṣaḥeeḥah*, hadith no. 430.

> "Allah has prohibited that you should swear by your fathers. If anyone swears, let him swear by Allah, or else remain silent."[16]

Ibn 'Umar (رضي الله عنه) also reported that the Prophet (ﷺ) said:

> "Whoever swears by something other than Allah is guilty of *ash-shirk*."[17]

The Prophet (ﷺ) said:

> "Whoever swears by trustworthiness is not one of us."[18]

It is not permitted to swear by the Ka'bah, by trustworthiness, by honour, by help, by the blessing of so-and-so, by the life of so-and-so, by the virtue of the Prophet (ﷺ), by the virtue of a *wali* (saint), by one's father and mother, by the heads of one's children, etc. All of that is *ḥarām*, and the expiation for doing it is to say, '*Lā ilāha illā Allah*', as is stated in the *ṣaḥeeḥ* hadith:

> "Whoever swears and says, 'By al-Lāt or By al-'Uzzā,' let him say, '*Lā ilāha illā Allah* (there is no true god except Allah)'."[19]

There are other phrases that similarly involve *shirk* and are therefore forbidden, but that are often spoken by Muslims, such as: "I seek refuge with Allah and with you", "I am depending on

---

[16] Bukhāri; see *Fatḥ al-Bāri*, 11/530.

[17] Aḥmad, 2/125; see *Ṣaḥeeḥ al-Jāmi'*, hadith no. 6204.

[18] Abu Dāwood, hadith no. 3253; see also *Silsilat al-aḥādeeth aṣ-Ṣaḥeeḥah*, hadith no. 94.

[19] Bukhāri, See *Fatḥ al-Bāri*, 11/536.

Allah and on you", "This is from Allah and from you", "I have no one but Allah and you", "I have Allah in heaven and I have you on earth", "If it were not for Allah and so-and-so", "I disown Islam", "Time has let me down", (and every other expression which involves cursing time, like saying, "This is a bad time", "This is an unlucky time", "Time is a betrayer" etc., because cursing time is an insult to Allah, Who has created time). Names that imply being a slave of anyone other than Allah, such as *'Abdul-Maseeḥ*, *'Abdun-Nabi*, *'Abdur-Rasool* and *'Abdul-Ḥusayn*, are also forbidden.

There are also modern expressions which are contrary to *Tawḥeed* and are therefore *ḥarām*, such as "Islamic socialism," "Islamic democracy", "The will of the people is the will of Allah", "Religion is for Allah and the land is for the people", "In the name of Arabism", "In the name of the revolution" etc.

It is also *ḥarām* to use titles such as "King of kings" or "Judge of judges" for human beings, to address *munafiqeen* (hypocrites) or *kuffār* with titles like "*Sayyid* (master)" (whether speaking Arabic or other languages), to use the words "If only..." — which imply discontent and regret and open the way for satan, and to say, "O' Allah! Forgive me if You want to."[20]

[20] For more information, see *Mu'jam al-Manāhi al-Lafdhiyyah* by Sheikh Bakr Abu Zayd.

8. Sitting with hypocrites and wrongdoers to enjoy their company or to keep them in company

Many of those who do not have strong faith deliberately sit with people who are immoral and sinful They may even sit with those who attack the *Sharee'ah* and make fun of Islam and the people who adhere to it strictly. There is no doubt that this is a forbidden deed, one which could undermine a person's belief. Allah (ﷻ) says:

﴿وَإِذَا رَأَيْتَ ٱلَّذِينَ يَخُوضُونَ فِىٓ ءَايَـٰتِنَا فَأَعْرِضْ عَنْهُمْ حَتَّىٰ يَخُوضُوا۟ فِى حَدِيثٍ غَيْرِهِۦ ۚ وَإِمَّا يُنسِيَنَّكَ ٱلشَّيْطَـٰنُ فَلَا تَقْعُدْ بَعْدَ ٱلذِّكْرَىٰ مَعَ ٱلْقَوْمِ ٱلظَّـٰلِمِينَ ﴿٦٨﴾﴾ (سورة الأنعام: ٦٨)

﴾And when you [Muhammad] see those who engage in a false conversation about Our Verses [of the Qur'an] stay away from them till they turn to another topic. And if satan causes you to forget, then after the remembrance do not sit in the company of those people who are the *Dhālimoon* [polytheists and wrongdoers].﴿ *(Qur'an 6: 68)*

In that case it is not permitted to sit with them, even if they are closely-related or are very kind and good company, except for the purposes of *Da'wah* (call to Islam) or for refuting their false talk. But accepting their conduct and remaining quiet about it is not permitted. Allah (ﷻ) says:

﴿... فَإِن تَرْضَوْا۟ عَنْهُمْ فَإِنَّ ٱللَّهَ لَا يَرْضَىٰ عَنِ ٱلْقَوْمِ ٱلْفَـٰسِقِينَ ﴿٩٦﴾﴾ (سورة التوبة: ٩٦)

﴿... but if you are pleased with them, certainly Allah is not pleased with the people who are *Fāsiqoon* [dissolute, disobedient to Allah].﴾ *(Qur'an 9: 96)*

9. Lack of composure in prayer

One of the worst forms of theft or cheating is cheating in prayer. The Messenger of Allah (ﷺ) said:

> "The worst type of thief is the one who steals from his prayer." The people asked, "O' Messenger of Allah! How can a person steal from his prayer?" He said: "By not doing *rukoo'* and *sujood* (bowing and prostrating) properly."[21]

This lack of composure and failure to pause in *rukoo'* and *sujood* or to stand up straight after *rukoo'* or sit up properly between *sujood* may be observed in many of those who pray, and hardly any mosque is free of examples of people who do not have the proper composure in prayer. Correct composure is one of the pillars of prayer, without which prayer is invalid. This is a serious matter. The Prophet (ﷺ) said:

> "A man's prayer is not good enough until his back is straight in *rukoo'* and *sujood*."[22]

There is no doubt that lacking the proper composure is bad, and the person who is guilty of this deserves to be reprimanded and threatened with punishment. Abu 'Abdullah al-Ash'ari (رضي الله عنه) reported that the Prophet (ﷺ) led his Companions in prayer, then

---

[21] Aḥmad, 5/310; see also *Ṣaḥeeḥ al-Jāmi'*, hadith no. 997.

[22] Abu Dāwood, 1/533; see also *Ṣaḥeeḥ al-Jāmi'*, hadith no. 7224.

he sat with a group of them. A man came in and started to pray, but made his movements rapid like a chicken pecking the ground. The Prophet (ﷺ) said:

> "Do you see this? Whoever dies having done this has died outside of the community of Muhammad, and his prayer is like a crow pecking blood. The person who bows then pecks in his *sujood* is like a hungry man who eats no more than one or two dates — what good will that do to him?"[23]

Zayd ibn Wahb said:

> "Ḥudhayfah saw a man who was not performing *rukoo'* and *sujood* properly." He said: 'You have not prayed, and if you were to die, you would die on a way other than that revealed by Allah to Prophet Muhammad.' "[24]

Once a person is aware of this ruling and he fails to perform prayer with the proper composure, he should repeat it and repent to Allah (ﷻ) of what is past; he does not need to repeat all of his previous prayers, as is indicated by the hadith:

> "Repeat your prayer, for you have not prayed."

---

[23] Ibn Khuzaymah in his *Ṣaḥeeḥ*, 1/332; see also al-Albāni, *Ṣifat Ṣalāt an-Nabi — The Prophet's Prayer described*, P. 131.

[24] Bukhāri, see *Fatḥ al-Bāri*, 2/274.

10. Fidgeting and making unnecessary movements in prayer

Hardly any of the people who pray are free from this problem, because they are not following the command of Allah.

﴿... وَقُومُوا۟ لِلَّهِ قَـٰنِتِينَ ﴿٢٣٨﴾﴾ (سورة البَقَـرَة: ٢٣٨)

﴿... And stand before Allah with obedience.﴾ *(Qur'an 2: 238)*

And they fail to understand such words of Allah (ﷻ).

﴿قَدْ أَفْلَحَ ٱلْمُؤْمِنُونَ ﴿١﴾ ٱلَّذِينَ هُمْ فِى صَلَاتِهِمْ خَـٰشِعُونَ ﴿٢﴾﴾ (سورة المؤمنون: ١-٢)

﴿Successful indeed are the believers. Those who offer their *Ṣalāt* [prayers] with all solemnity and full submissiveness.﴾ *(Qur'an 23: 1-2)*

When the Prophet (ﷺ) was asked about smoothing the earth before prostrating, he said:

> "Do not wipe it when you are praying; if you have to, then just smooth the gravel once."[25]

The scholars mentioned that continuous, excessive, unnecessary movement invalidates one's prayer. How can those fidgets stand before Allah (ﷻ) looking at their watches, straightening their clothes, putting their fingers in their noses, looking to the right and the left and up to the sky, and not fearing

---

[25] Abu Dāwood, 1/581; see also *Ṣaḥeeḥ al-Jāmi'*, hadith no. 7452.

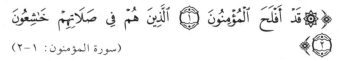

that Allah may take away their sight or satan may steal their prayer?

11. Deliberately anticipating the movements of the Imam (when praying in congregation)

Man is hasty by nature, as it says in the Qur'an:

﴿... وَكَانَ ٱلْإِنسَٰنُ عَجُولًا ﴿١١﴾﴾ (سورة الإسراء: ١١)

﴾... and man is ever hasty.﴿ *(Qur'an 17: 11)*

The Prophet (ﷺ) said:

> "Deliberation is from Allah and haste is from satan."[26]

When praying in congregation, one often notices people to the left and right anticipating the Imam in *rukoo', sujood* and the *takbeerāt* that signal changes in position — one even notices it in oneself sometimes. People may even precede the Imam in giving *as-salām* at the end of the prayer. This is a matter which may appear unimportant to many, but the Prophet (ﷺ) issued a stern warning when He (ﷺ) said:

> "Does the person who raises his head before the Imam not fear that Allah may turn his head into the head of a donkey?"[27]

If a person is required to come to the prayer with dignity and composure, how then should he be during the prayer itself?

---

[26] Al-Bayhaqi, *as-Sunan al-Kubrā*, 10/104; see also *Silsilat al-aḥādeeth aṣ-Ṣaḥeeḥah*, hadith no. 1795.

[27] Muslim, 1/320-321.

Some people are confused about this issue and seek to compensate by delaying their movements after the Imam; these people should know that the *fuqahā'* (jurists), may Allah have mercy on them, have described an excellent way to control the matter: They said that the person following the Imam should only start his movements after the Imam has finished pronouncing the *ra'* ('r') of '*Allahu akbar*'; then the person following the Imam is permitted to move, and not before or after. The Companions of the Prophet used to be very keen to avoid anticipating his movements when he led them in prayer. One of them, al-Barā' ibn 'Āzib (رضي الله عنه) said that they used to pray behind the Prophet (ﷺ):

> "When he raised his head from *rukoo'*, I would never see anyone bending his back in *sujood* until the Messenger of Allah had placed his forehead on the ground, then everyone would go down in *sujood* behind him."[28]

When the Prophet (ﷺ) grew older, and became rather slow in his movements, he told the people praying behind him:

> "O' people! I have gained weight, so do not anticipate me in performing *rukoo'* and *sujood*."[29]

The Imam is obliged to follow the *Sunnah* in making *takbeer* when he prays, as reported in the hadith narrated by Abu Hurayrah (رضي الله عنه):

> "When the Messenger of Allah stood up to pray, he would say *takbeer* (saying: "*Allahu Akbar*") when he stood up and when he bowed... then he would say

---

[28] Muslim, hadith no. 474, 'Abdul-Bāqi edition.

[29] Al-Bayhaqi, 2/93 and classified as *ḥasan* in *Irwā' al-Ghaleel*, 2/290.

> *takbeer* when he went down for *sujood* and when he raised his head, then when he went down for *sujood* again and when he raised his head again. Then he would repeat this throughout the whole prayer until it was finished, and he would say *takbeer* when he stood up after completing two *rak'ahs*."[30]

If the Imam pronounces *takbeer* at the same time as he makes the movements, and the people following him strive to follow the guidelines mentioned here, then they will have performed the congregational prayer correctly.

12. Coming to the mosque after eating onions or garlic, or anything that has an offensive smell

Allah (ﷻ) says:

> ﴿يَـٰبَنِىٓ ءَادَمَ خُذُوا۟ زِينَتَكُمْ عِندَ كُلِّ مَسْجِدٍ﴾ (سورة الأعراف: ٣١)
>
> ﴾O' Children of Adam! Take your adornment [by wearing your clean clothes], at every *masjid* (place of prayer)...﴿ *(Qur'an 7: 31)*

Jābir (رضي الله عنه) said: "The Messenger of Allah (ﷺ) said:

> 'Whoever eats garlic or onions, let him keep away from us,' or 'let him keep away from our mosque and stay in his house.''[31]

---

[30] Bukhāri, hadith no. 756, al-Baghā edition.

[31] Bukhāri, see *Fatḥ al-Bāri*, 2/339,

According to a report narrated by Muslim, the Prophet (ﷺ) said:

> "Whoever eats onions, garlic or leeks, let him not come near our mosque, because the angels will be offended by what is offensive to the sons of Adam."[32]

'Umar ibn al-Khaṭṭāb (رضي الله عنه) addressed the people one Friday and said:

> "O' people! You eat two things that I think come from bad plants: onions and garlic. When the Messenger of Allah (ﷺ) noticed this smell coming from a man in the mosque, he ordered him to go out to *al-Baqee'* (a cemetery in Madeenah). Whoever wants to eat these things, let him cook them to death."[33]

We might also include here those who come to the mosque straight from work, with unpleasant odours emanating from their armpits and socks. Even worse than these are smokers who have the habit of consuming their *ḥarām* cigarettes then coming to the mosque and disturbing the worshippers of Allah, people and angels alike, with their smell.

13. *Az-Zinā* — Fornication and adultery

One of the aims of Islamic *Sharee'ah* is to preserve honour and lineage, so *az-zinā* (unlawful sexual intercourse) is forbidden. Allah (سبحانه وتعالى) says:

---

[32] Muslim, 1/395.

[33] Ibid, 1/396.

﴿وَلَا تَقْرَبُوا۟ ٱلزِّنَىٰٓ ۖ إِنَّهُۥ كَانَ فَٰحِشَةً وَسَآءَ سَبِيلًا ﴿٣٢﴾﴾

(سورة الإسراء: ٣٢)

﴾And come not near to unlawful sexual intercourse. Verily, it is a *Fāḥishah* [a great sin], and an evil way [that leads one to Hell unless Allah forgives him].﴿ *(Qur'an 17: 32)*

Sharee'ah blocks all the ways and means that could lead to *az-zinā*, by enjoining *ḥijāb* (Islamic dress) and lowering the gaze, and by forbidding being alone with a non-*maḥram* (marriageable) woman, etc.

The married man who commits adultery deserves the worst kind of punishment, which is stoning to death, so that he may taste the results of his deeds and so that every part of his body may suffer just as every part of his body enjoyed the illicit liaison. The fornicator who was previously unmarried is to be punished with the maximum number of lashes mentioned in *Sharee'ah*, which is one hundred lashes, in addition to the scandal of this punishment being witnessed by a group of believers, and the humiliation of being banished from his city and the scene of his crime for one full year.

In *al-Barzakh* (phase between death and resurrection), the punishment for men and women who were guilty of *az-zinā* is that they will be in an oven whose top is narrow and whose bottom is wide, with a fire beneath it, and they will be naked therein. When the heat of the fire increases, they will scream and rise up until they nearly come out of the top, then when the fire decreases, they will fall back down. This will be repeated over and over until the onset of the Hour.

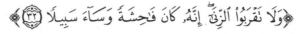

What is even worse is when a man continues to commit adultery even when he grows old and approaches death, and Allah (ﷻ) gives him the opportunity to repent. Abu Hurayrah (رضي الله عنه) reported that the Prophet (ﷺ) said:

> "There are three to whom Allah will not speak on the Day of Resurrection, nor vindicate, nor look at, and theirs will be a painful torment: an old man who commits *zinā*, a king who lies, and a poor man who is arrogant."[34]

> "Among the worst of incomes is the earnings of a prostitute which she takes for committing *zinā*, and the immoral woman who earns her living by selling herself is deprived of having her prayers answered when the gates of heaven are opened at midnight."[35]

Being in need and being poor are not acceptable excuses for transgressing the limits set by Allah (ﷻ). There is an old saying that the free woman would rather starve than eat by displaying her breasts, so how about her private parts then?

Nowadays, all the doors of immorality have been opened, and satan and his supporters have made it very easy for people to commit sin. This has been followed by the spread of *tabarruj* (wanton display) and unveiling among women, people allowing their gazes to wander to things they should not look at, an increase in mixing between the sexes, the popularity of immoral magazines and lewd films, increased travel to corrupt countries and the establishment of a market for prostitution, an increase in the

---

[34] Muslim, 1/102-103.

[35] *Ṣaḥeeḥ al-Jāmi'*, hadith no. 2971.

violation of honour and an increase in the number of illegitimate births and abortions.

O' Allah! We ask you to show us Your mercy, protect us from immorality, purify our hearts and keep our private parts chaste and placc a barrier between us and what is *ḥarām*, *Āmeen*.

14. Sodomy (Homosexuality)

Sodomy, or intercourse between two males, was the crime of the people of Prophet Lot (عليه السلام) (may peace be upon him). Allah (سبحانه وتعالى) says:

﴿وَلُوطًا إِذْ قَالَ لِقَوْمِهِۦٓ إِنَّكُمْ لَتَأْتُونَ ٱلْفَٰحِشَةَ مَا
سَبَقَكُم بِهَا مِنْ أَحَدٍ مِّنَ ٱلْعَٰلَمِينَ ﴿٢٨﴾ أَئِنَّكُمْ لَتَأْتُونَ
ٱلرِّجَالَ وَتَقْطَعُونَ ٱلسَّبِيلَ وَتَأْتُونَ فِى نَادِيكُمُ ٱلْمُنكَرَ
... ﴿٢٩﴾﴾ (سورة العَنكبوت: ٢٨-٢٩)

﴾And [remember] Lot, when he said to his people: 'You commit *al-Fāḥishah* [sodomy] which none has preceded you to from among the *'Ālameen* [worlds, mankind and jinn]. Verily, you commit sodomy with men, and rob the wayfarer, and practise *al-Munkar* [every kind of evil] in your meetings.'...﴿

(Qur'an 29: 28-29)

Because of the repulsive nature and enormity of this sin, Allah (سبحانه وتعالى) inflicted a combination of four kinds of punishment which He had never inflicted before upon any other people: they were blinded, their city was turned upside-down, stones of baked clay were piled up and rained down upon them and a thunderous cry overtook them.

In Islam, those guilty of this crime are to be killed by the sword, according to the soundest opinion. This punishment is to be carried out on both the one who does this and the one to whom it is done, if it is done freely and by choice. Ibn 'Abbās (رضي الله عنه) reported that the Prophet (ﷺ) said:

> "Whomever you find committing the sin of the people of Lot, kill them — both the one who does it and the one to whom it is done."[36]

The recent spread of incurable diseases, that were unknown to our predecessors, like the killer AIDS caused by this corruption, is an indication of the wisdom of the *Sharee'ah* in prescribing this severe punishment.

15. Wife denying marital relation without valid reason

Abu Hurayrah (رضي الله عنه) reported that the Prophet (ﷺ) said:

> "If a man calls his wife to his bed and she refuses, and he goes to sleep angry with her, the angels will curse her until morning."[37]

Many women, when they have an argument with their husbands, "punish" them — as they think — by denying them their marital rights. This may result in major corruption if the husband is tempted to do something *ḥarām*, or it may backfire on the wife if the husband starts thinking seriously of taking another wife.

---

[36] Aḥmad, 1/300; see also *Ṣaḥeeḥ al-Jāmi'*, hadith no. 6565.

[37] Bukhāri; see *Fatḥ al-Bāri*, 6/314.

A wife should hasten to respond to her husband's call if he wants her, in obedience to the words of the Prophet (ﷺ):

> "If a man calls his wife to his bed, let her respond, even if she is riding on the back of a camel (i.e., very busy)."[38]

At the same time, the husband must show consideration towards his wife if she is sick, pregnant or depressed, so as to maintain harmony and prevent discontent or hatred.

16. Wife demanding divorce for no valid reason

Many women hasten to demand divorce from their husbands for the least argument, or if their husbands do not give them what they want of money. Some women may be misled by troublemakers among their relatives or neighbours to challenge their husbands with provocative words such as: "If you were a real man, you would divorce me!" The dire results of divorce are well-known; breakdown of the family and children roaming the streets. A person may come to regret divorce when it is too late. For all these reasons and others, the *Sharee'ah* wisely prohibited such actions. Thawbān (رضي الله عنه) reported that the Prophet (ﷺ) said:

> "Any woman who asks her husband for divorce with no sound reason will be deprived of smelling the fragrance of Paradise."[39]

---

[38] See *Zawā'id al-Bazzār*, 2/181; see also *Ṣaḥeeḥ al-Jāmi'*, hadith no. 547.

[39] Aḥmad, 5/277; see also *Ṣaḥeeḥ al-Jāmi'*, hadith no. 2703.

'Uqbah ibn 'Āmir (رضي الله عنه) reported that the Prophet (ﷺ) said:

> "Women who ask for divorce and women who quarrel with their husbands are hypocrites."[40]

But if there is a sound reason, such as the husband abandoning prayer, drinking or taking drugs, or forcing his wife to do something *ḥarām*, or oppressing her and making her suffer by denying her the rights granted to her by Islam, and he does not listen to advice to mend his ways, then there is nothing wrong with a woman seeking divorce for her own sake and for the sake of her religion.

17. *Adh-Dhihār*

One of the expressions of the first *Jāhiliyyah*, still widespread in this *Ummah* (nation), is the phenomenon of *adh-Dhihār*, whereby a man says to his wife, "You are to me like the back of my mother", or "You are as forbidden for me as my sister," or other similar ugly statements. Such utterances are denounced by the *Sharee'ah*, as they entail oppression and tyranny against women. Allah (سبحانه وتعالى) referred to this in the Qur'an:

> ﴿ٱلَّذِينَ يُظَٰهِرُونَ مِنكُم مِّن نِّسَآئِهِم مَّا هُنَّ أُمَّهَٰتِهِمۡۖ إِنۡ أُمَّهَٰتُهُمۡ إِلَّا ٱلَّٰٓـِٔي وَلَدۡنَهُمۡۚ وَإِنَّهُمۡ لَيَقُولُونَ مُنكَرٗا مِّنَ ٱلۡقَوۡلِ وَزُورٗاۚ وَإِنَّ ٱللَّهَ لَعَفُوٌّ غَفُورٞ ٢﴾ (سورة المجادلة: ٢)

> ﴿Those among you who make their wives unlawful to them by *adh-Dhihār* [i.e. saying to them, 'You are like my mother's back']; they (wives) cannot be their

[40] Aṭ-Ṭabarāni in *al-Kabeer*, 17/339; see also *Ṣaḥeeḥ al-Jāmi'*, hadith no. 1934.

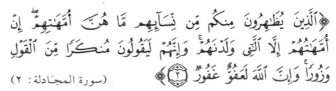

mothers. None can be their mothers except those who gave them birth. And verily, they utter an ill word and a lie. But indeed, Allah is Oft-Pardoning, Oft-Forgiving.﴾ *(Qur'an 58: 2)*

The *Sharee'ah* has imposed a heavy penalty (*kaffārah mughalladhah*) for this crime, similar to that required for killing a person by mistake or for having intercourse during the day in Ramaḍān (while fasting); the person who has committed *adh-Dhihār* is not permitted to approach his wife until he has paid this penalty. Allah (ﷻ) says:

﴿وَٱلَّذِينَ يُظَٰهِرُونَ مِن نِّسَآئِهِمْ ثُمَّ يَعُودُونَ لِمَا قَالُوا۟ فَتَحْرِيرُ رَقَبَةٍ مِّن قَبْلِ أَن يَتَمَآسَّا ۚ ذَٰلِكُمْ تُوعَظُونَ بِهِۦ ۚ وَٱللَّهُ بِمَا تَعْمَلُونَ خَبِيرٌ ﴿٣﴾ فَمَن لَّمْ يَجِدْ فَصِيَامُ شَهْرَيْنِ مُتَتَابِعَيْنِ مِن قَبْلِ أَن يَتَمَآسَّا ۖ فَمَن لَّمْ يَسْتَطِعْ فَإِطْعَامُ سِتِّينَ مِسْكِينًا ۚ ذَٰلِكَ لِتُؤْمِنُوا۟ بِٱللَّهِ وَرَسُولِهِۦ ۚ وَتِلْكَ حُدُودُ ٱللَّهِ ۗ وَلِلْكَٰفِرِينَ عَذَابٌ أَلِيمٌ ﴿٤﴾﴾

(سورة المجادلة: ٣-٤)

﴾And those who make their wives unlawful to them by *Dhihār* and wish to free themselves from what they uttered, [the penalty] in that case is the freeing of a slave before they touch each other. That is an admonition to you [so that you may not return to such an ill thing]. And Allah is All-Aware of what you do. And he who finds not [the money for freeing a slave] must fast two successive months before they both touch each other. And for him who is unable to do so, he should feed sixty *miskeen* [poor]. That is in order that you may have perfect Faith in Allah and His Messenger. And those are the limits [set] by Allah.

And for disbelievers, there is a painful torment.﴿

(Qur'an 58: 3-4)

18. Sex with wife during menses

Allah (ﷻ) says:

﴿وَيَسْـَٔلُونَكَ عَنِ ٱلْمَحِيضِ ۖ قُلْ هُوَ أَذًى فَٱعْتَزِلُوا۟ ٱلنِّسَآءَ فِى ٱلْمَحِيضِ ۖ وَلَا تَقْرَبُوهُنَّ حَتَّىٰ يَطْهُرْنَ ... ﴿٢٢٢﴾﴾

(سورة البَقَـرَة: ٢٢٢)

﴾They ask you about menstruation. Say: that is an *adhā* [a harmful thing for a husband to have sexual intercourse with his wife while she is having her menses], therefore keep away from women during menses and go not unto them till they are purified [from menses and have taken a bath]...﴿

(Qur'an 2: 222)

So a man is not permitted to approach his wife until her period has ended and she has taken a bath (*ghusl*). Allah (ﷻ) says:

﴿... فَإِذَا تَطَهَّرْنَ فَأْتُوهُنَّ مِنْ حَيْثُ أَمَرَكُمُ ٱللَّهُ ۚ ... ﴿٢٢٢﴾﴾

(سورة البَقَـرَة: ٢٢٢)

﴾... And when they have purified themselves, then go in unto them as Allah has ordained for you...﴿

(Qur'an 2: 222)

The repulsive nature of this sin is indicated by the words of the Prophet (ﷺ):

"Whoever has intercourse with a menstruating woman, or with a woman in her rectum, or goes to a

> fortune-teller, has disbelieved in what is revealed to Muhammad."[41]

Whoever does this by mistake, not deliberately, does not have to pay any penalty, but the person who does it deliberately and with full knowledge of what he is doing must pay the penalty, which according to the scholars with the soundest knowledge is one dinar or half a dinar. Some scholars are of the opinion that there is a choice in the amount to be paid; others say that if a man has intercourse with his wife at the beginning of her period, when the flow of blood is heavy, he must pay one dinar, and if he does it at the end of her period when the flow is light, he must pay half a dinar. In modern terms, a dinar is equal to 4.25 grams of gold: this, or the equivalent amount of currency must be given in charity.

19. Having intercourse with one's wife in her rectum

Some perverted people who have little faith do not hesitate to have intercourse with a woman in her rectum (the place from which feces are discharged). This is a major sin, and the Prophet (ﷺ) cursed the one who does this. Abu Hurayrah (رضي الله عنه) reported that the Prophet (ﷺ) said:

> "He is cursed, the one who has intercourse with a woman in her rectum."[42]

---

[41] At-Tirmidhi from Abu Hurayrah (رضي الله عنه), 1/243; see also *Ṣaḥeeḥ al-Jāmi'*, hadith no. 5918.

[42] Aḥmad, 2/479; see also *Ṣaḥeeḥ al-Jāmi'*, hadith no. 5865.

Indeed, the Prophet (ﷺ) said:

> "Whoever has intercourse with a menstruating woman, or with a woman in her rectum, or goes to a fortune-teller, has disbelieved in what is revealed to Muhammad."[43]

Although there are many righteous and sensible women who refuse to do this, there are many husbands who threaten their wives with divorce if they do not comply. Some husbands even deceive their wives who may be too shy to ask a scholar about this matter; they tell them that this is *ḥalāl*, and they may even misquote the Qur'an to support their claim:

﴿نِسَآؤُكُمْ حَرْثٌ لَّكُمْ فَأْتُوا۟ حَرْثَكُمْ أَنَّىٰ شِئْتُمْ ... ﴿٢٢٣﴾﴾

(سورة البَقَرَة: ٢٢٣)

> ﴾Your wives are a tilth for you, so go to your tilth when or how you will,...﴿ *(Qur'an 2: 223)*

But it is well-known that the *Sunnah* explains the Qur'an, and the Prophet (ﷺ) stated that it is permitted to have intercourse with one's wife in whatever way one wishes, approaching from the front or the back, so long as intercourse is in the place from which a child is born (the vagina); it is obvious that the anus, from which stool is passed, is not the place from which a child is born. One of the reasons for this crime is the fact that many people enter what should be a clean and pure married life with an inheritance of dirty, *ḥarām* (unlawful), *jāhili* (pre-Islamic), perverted practices, or memories filled with scenes from lewd movies of which they

---

[43] At-Tirmidhi from Abu Hurayrah, 1/243; see also *Ṣaḥeeḥ al-Jāmi'*, hadith no. 5918.

have not repented to Allah (سبحانه وتعالى). It is also well-known that this deed is *ḥarām* even if both parties consent to it; mutual consent to a *ḥarām* deed does not make it *ḥalāl*.

20. Injustice with co-wives

One of the things that Allah has enjoined in His Book is fair and equal treatment with co-wives. Allah (سبحانه وتعالى) says:

﴿وَلَن تَسْتَطِيعُوٓا۟ أَن تَعْدِلُوا۟ بَيْنَ ٱلنِّسَآءِ وَلَوْ حَرَصْتُمْ ۖ فَلَا
تَمِيلُوا۟ كُلَّ ٱلْمَيْلِ فَتَذَرُوهَا كَٱلْمُعَلَّقَةِ ۚ وَإِن تُصْلِحُوا۟
وَتَتَّقُوا۟ فَإِنَّ ٱللَّهَ كَانَ غَفُورًا رَّحِيمًا ﴿١٢٩﴾﴾

(سورة النِّسَاء: ١٢٩)

﴿You will never be able to do perfect justice among wives even if it is your ardent desire, so do not incline too much [to one of them (by giving her more of your time and provision)] so as to leave the other hanging [i.e. neither divorced nor married]. And if you do justice, and do all that is right and fear Allah by keeping away from all that is wrong, then Allah is Ever Oft-Forgiving, All-Merciful.﴾ *(Qur'an 4: 129)*

The justice required here is a fair (and equal) division of nights, and the giving of each wife her rights as regards spending and clothing. This does not refer to emotions or love, because man has no control over his feelings. But when some people marry more than one wife they favour one and neglect the other, spending more time with and more money on one wife and ignoring the other. This is *ḥarām*, and the person who does this will come on the Day of Resurrection in the condition described by the Prophet (ﷺ) in the hadith narrated by Abu Hurayrah (رضي الله عنه):

> "Whoever has two wives and gives one of them preferential treatment, will come on the Day of Resurrection with half of his body leaning."[44]

21. Being alone with a non-*maḥram* woman

Satan is always keen to tempt people and make them commit *ḥarām* deeds. For this reason, Allah (سبحانه وتعالى) warned us:

> ﴿يَٰٓأَيُّهَا ٱلَّذِينَ ءَامَنُواْ لَا تَتَّبِعُواْ خُطُوَٰتِ ٱلشَّيۡطَٰنِۚ وَمَن يَتَّبِعۡ خُطُوَٰتِ ٱلشَّيۡطَٰنِ فَإِنَّهُۥ يَأۡمُرُ بِٱلۡفَحۡشَآءِ وَٱلۡمُنكَرِۚ ... ﴿٢١﴾﴾
>
> (سورة النُّور: ٢١)
>
> ﴿O' you who believe! Follow not the footsteps of *satan*. And whosoever follows the footsteps of *satan*, then, verily he commands [committing] *al-Faḥshā'* [indecency] and *al-Munkar* [evil deeds]...﴾
>
> *(Qur'an 24: 21)*

Satan runs through the veins of mankind like blood, and one of the ways in which he induces people to commit indecent acts is by leading a man to be alone with a non-*maḥram* woman. Islam blocks this way by forbidding such conduct, as the Prophet (ﷺ) said:

> "No man is alone with a (non-*maḥram*) woman, but satan will be the third among them."[45]

---

[44] Abu Dāwood, 2/601; see also *Ṣaḥeeḥ al-Jāmi'*, hadith no. 6491.

[45] At-Tirmidhi, 3/474; see also *Mishkāt al-Maṣābeeḥ*, hadith no. 3118.

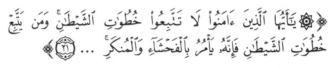

Ibn 'Umar (رضي الله عنه) reported that the Prophet (ﷺ) said:

> "From this day on, no man should visit a woman
> whose husband is absent unless there is another man
> or two with him."[46]

It is not permitted for a man to be alone in a house, room or
car with a non-*mahram* woman, including his brother's wife or a
[female] servant. Similarly, a female patient should not be alone
with a doctor, and so on. Many people are careless about this
matter, whether because they trust themselves or for some other
reason, with the result that many commit indecent acts or take the
steps that lead to them, which in turn results in the tragedies of
confused lineage and illegitimate births.

22. Shaking hands with a non-*mahram* woman

This is one of the cases where incorrect social customs have
taken precedence over the laws of Allah (ﷻ), to such an extent
that if you try to talk to people and show them evidence that this is
wrong, they will accuse you of being backward, having a
complex, trying to break family ties, doubting their good
intentions, etc. Shaking hands with female cousins, brothers'
wives and uncles' wives is now easier than drinking water in our
society. But if we look properly, we will understand the
seriousness of the matter. The Prophet (ﷺ) said:

> "If one of you were to be stabbed in the head with an
> iron needle, it would be better for him than touching a
> woman whom he is not permitted to touch."[47]

---

[46] Muslim, 4/1711.

[47] At-Ṭabarāni, 20/212; see also *Ṣaḥeeḥ al-Jāmi'*, hadith no. 4921.

There is no doubt that this is an act of *zinā* (fornication), because the Prophet (ﷺ) said:

> "The eyes may commit *zinā*, the hands may commit *zinā*, the feet may commit *zinā* and the private parts may commit *zinā*."[48]

Is there anyone more pure in heart than Muhammad (ﷺ)? And yet he said,

> "I do not shake hands with women."[49]
> And he (ﷺ) also said,
> "I do not touch the hands of women."[50]

'Ā'ishah[51] (رضي الله عنها) (may Allah be pleased with her), said:

> "No, by Allah, the hand of the Messenger of Allah never touched the hand of a (non-*maḥram*) woman. He received *Bay'ah* (pledge of allegiance) from them by word only."[52]

Let them fear Allah (ﷻ), who threaten their pious wives with divorce if they do not shake hands with their brothers.

We should also note that placing a barrier, such as a piece of cloth, is of no use; it is still *ḥarām* to shake hands with a non-*maḥram* woman.

---

48 Aḥmad, 1/412; see also *Ṣaḥeeḥ al-Jāmi'*, hadith no. 4126.

49 Imam Aḥmad, 6/357; see also *Ṣaḥeeḥ al-Jāmi'*, hadith no. 2509.

50 At-Tabarāni in *al-Kabeer*, 24/342; see also *Ṣaḥeeḥ al-Jāmi'*, hadith no. 7054 and *al-Iṣābah*, 4/354, Dār al-Kitāb al-'Arabi edition.

51 A wife of the Prophet and mother of the believers — daughter of Abu Bakr the first Caliph. Born in Makkah in 614 CE / 9 years before *Hijrah* and died in 678 CE / 58 AH in Madeenah, a renowned early scholar.

52 Muslim, 3/1489.

23. Woman wearing perfume when going out

This practice is widespread nowadays, despite the stern warning of the Prophet (ﷺ), who said:

> "Any woman who applies perfume and then goes out among the people so that they could smell her fragrance is a *zāniyah* (adulteress)."[53]

Some women are very careless and take the matter too lightly, especially in front of drivers, shopkeepers, school porters, etc., even though the *Sharee'ah* states very strictly that the woman who wears perfume must wash herself like a person must wash when in a state of *Janābah* (i.e., perform *ghusl* from sexual contact), if she wants to go out to the mosque. The Prophet (ﷺ) said:

> "Any woman who wears perfume then goes out to the mosque so that the fragrance can be discerned, her prayers will not be accepted until she performs *ghusl* like the *ghusl* performed when in a state of *janābah*."[54]

We complain to Allah about the *bakhoor* and *'ood* (types of burned incense) used at weddings and women's parties before people leave, and the use of strong-smelling perfumes in market-places, means of transportation and mixed gatherings and even in the mosques during the nights of Ramaḍān. Islam tells us that women's perfume should be that which has colour but little smell. We ask Allah (ﷻ) not to despise us and not to punish righteous

---

[53] Aḥmad, 4/418; see also *Ṣaḥeeḥ al-Jāmi'*, hadith no. 105.

[54] Imam Aḥmad, 2/444; see also *Ṣaḥeeḥ al-Jāmi'*, hadith no. 2703.

men and women for the deeds of foolish men and women. May He guide us all to the Straight Path.

24. A woman travelling without a *maḥram*

Bukhāri and Muslim reported from Ibn 'Abbās (رضي الله عنه) that the Messenger of Allah (ﷺ) said:

> "A woman should not travel save and except with a *maḥram*."[55]

This is a general instruction for all types of travels including that for *Ḥajj*.

A woman travelling without a *maḥram* encourages corrupt people to prey on her because of her weakness; at the very least, her honour will be harmed. This prohibition applies also to a woman travelling by plane, even if — as is often claimed — one *maḥram* sees her off at one end and another *maḥram* meets her at the other. Who is going to sit next to her during the journey? What if technical problems divert the plane to another airport, or the flight is delayed? What if...? There are too many stories of things that went wrong. For a person to be considered a *maḥram*, he must meet four conditions: he should be a Muslim, over the age of puberty, of sound mind, and male as per the hadith narrated by Abu Sa'eed al-Khudri (رضي الله عنه) that the Messenger of Allah (ﷺ) said:

> "No woman who believes in Allah and the Last Day should travel a distance of three days' journey or more unless her father, son, husband, brother or other *maḥram* is with her."[56]

---

[55] Muslim.

[56] Muslim.

Yet, in another hadith the Messenger of Allah (ﷺ) said:

> "It is not permitted for the woman who believes in Allah and the Last Day to travel one day's distance without the presence of a *maḥram*."[57]

25. Deliberately looking at a non-*maḥram* woman

Allah (ﷻ) says:

﴿قُل لِّلْمُؤْمِنِينَ يَغُضُّوا مِنْ أَبْصَارِهِمْ وَيَحْفَظُوا فُرُوجَهُمْ ذَٰلِكَ أَزْكَىٰ لَهُمْ إِنَّ اللَّهَ خَبِيرٌ بِمَا يَصْنَعُونَ ﴿٣٠﴾﴾ (سورة النُّور: ٣٠)

> ﴿Tell the believing men to lower their gaze [from looking at forbidden things], and to protect their private parts [from illegal sexual acts, etc.]. That is purer for them. Verily, Allah is All-Aware of what they do.﴾ *(Qur'an 24: 30)*

The Prophet (ﷺ) said:

> "The adultery of the eyes is by looking (i.e. by looking at what Allah has forbidden)."[58]

Looking for a legitimate purpose is exempted from this rule, such as looking at a woman for marriage purposes, or a doctor examining a patient for medical reasons, etc. Women are equally forbidden to look at non-*maḥram* men, as Allah (ﷻ) says:

---

[57] Ibid.

[58] Bukhāri, see *Fatḥ al-Bāri*, 11/26.

﴿وَقُل لِّلْمُؤْمِنَٰتِ يَغْضُضْنَ مِنْ أَبْصَٰرِهِنَّ وَيَحْفَظْنَ فُرُوجَهُنَّ ... ﴿٣١﴾﴾ (سورة النُّور: ٣١)

﴿And tell the believing women to lower their gaze [from looking at forbidden things], and protect their private parts [from illegal sexual acts, etc]...﴾ *(Qur'an 24: 31)*

Men are also forbidden to look with desire at a man with a hairless or beautiful face. Men are forbidden to look at the *'awrah* of other men (the parts between the navel and the knees), and women are forbidden to look at the *'awrah* of other women (also the parts between the navel and the knees — in the case of women to women). If it is forbidden to look at something, it is forbidden to touch it, even over clothing. One of the ways in which satan deceives people is by making them think that there is nothing wrong with looking at pictures in magazines or watching movies, because what is seen is not "real," even though such images clearly cause so much damage by provoking desires.

26. Seeing one's womenfolk behaving in an immoral fashion and keeping silent

Ibn 'Umar (رضي الله عنه) reported that the Prophet (ﷺ) said:

> "There are three whom Allah will deprive of Paradise: the one who drinks intoxicants, the one who is disobedient to his parents, and the one who accepts immoral conduct on the part of his family."[59]

[59] Aḥmad, 2/69; see also *Ṣaḥeeḥ al-Jāmi'*, hadith no. 3047.

One of the many examples of this in modern times is men turning a blind eye to their daughters or wives contacting non-*maḥram* men and chatting to them in a way that may be described as "romantic", or accepting one of the women of their household being alone with a non-*maḥram* man, or allowing her to sit alone with a driver or another employee, or letting her go out without proper *hijab* (women's Islamic dress), so that everyone may look at her, or bringing home immoral magazines and movies.

27. Making false claims about a child's lineage, or denying one's own child

According to *Sharee'ah*, it is not permissible for a Muslim to claim to belong to anyone other than his father, or to claim to belong to a family of whom he is not a member. Some people may do this for material gains, and may obtain documentation to "confirm" officially their false identity. Some people may do this out of hatred towards a father who abandoned them when they were children. All of this is *ḥarām*, and may lead to much chaos and corruption in a number of fields, such as knowing who is one's *maḥram*, marriage, inheritance and so on. Sa'd and Abu Bakrah (رضي الله عنهما) both reported that the Prophet (ﷺ) said:

> "Whoever knowingly claims to belong to anyone other than his father, Paradise will be denied to him."[60]

It is also forbidden to tamper with lineages or make false claims about a person's descent. There are some people who, when they want to fight in dirty arguments with their wives,

---

[60] Bukhāri; see *Fatḥ al-Bāri*, 8/45.

accuse them of immoral conduct and disown their children, without any proof, when the child was born "in their bed" (i.e. is the husband's child and no one else's). There are also some wives who betray their trust and become pregnant with other men's children, but claim that they belong to their husbands. The Prophet (ﷺ) issued a stern warning against such conduct. Abu Hurayrah (رضي الله عنه) reported that when *āyat al-mulā'anah* (*an-Noor* 24: 7) was revealed,

﴿وَٱلْخَٰمِسَةُ أَنَّ لَعْنَتَ ٱللَّهِ عَلَيْهِ إِن كَانَ مِنَ ٱلْكَٰذِبِينَ ۝٧﴾

(سورة النُّور: ٧)

﴿And the fifth [testimony should be] the invoking of the Curse of Allah on him if he be of those who tell a lie [against her].﴾ *(Qur'an 24: 7)*

The Prophet (ﷺ) said:

> "The woman who brings into a people someone who does not belong to them has nothing to do with Allah, and Allah will not admit her to Paradise. Any man who denies his own child when he is looking at him, Allah will not show Himself to him and will expose him before all people."[61]

28. Consuming *ribā* (Usury)

In the Qur'an, Allah (ﷻ) does not declare war on anyone except the people who deal with *ribā*.

---

[61] Abu Dāwood, 2/695; see also *Mishkāt al-Maṣābeeḥ*, hadith no. 3316.

﴿يَـٰٓأَيُّهَا ٱلَّذِينَ ءَامَنُوا۟ ٱتَّقُوا۟ ٱللَّهَ وَذَرُوا۟ مَا بَقِىَ مِنَ ٱلرِّبَوٰٓا۟ إِن كُنتُم مُّؤْمِنِينَ ﴿٢٧٨﴾ فَإِن لَّمْ تَفْعَلُوا۟ فَأْذَنُوا۟ بِحَرْبٍ مِّنَ ٱللَّهِ وَرَسُولِهِۦ ... ﴿٢٧٩﴾﴾

(سورة البَقَـرَة: ٢٧٨-٢٧٩)

﴿O' you who believe! Be afraid of Allah and give up what remains [due to you] from *riba* [usury] [from now onward], if you are [really] believers. And if you do not do it, then take a notice of war from Allah and His Messenger...﴾ *(Qur'an 2: 278-279)*

This is sufficient to explain the abhorrence of this deed in the sight of Allah, be He glorified.

One may easily discern the extent of devastation, at the individual and international levels, caused by dealing with *ribā* — such as bankruptcy, recession, economic stagnation, inability to repay loans, high unemployment, collapse of many companies and institutions, etc. Daily toil has become a never-ending struggle to pay off interest on loans and societies have become class-ridden structures in which huge wealth is concentrated in the hands of a few. Perhaps all this is a manifestation of the war threatened by Allah (ﷻ) to those who deal with *ribā*.

Everyone who has something to do with *ribā*, whether he is one of the main parties involved or a middleman or facilitator, has been cursed by the Prophet. Jābir (رضي الله عنه) reported that the Messenger of Allah, (ﷺ), said:

> "Cursed be the one who consumes *ribā*, the one who gives it to others, the one who writes it down and the one who witnesses it." He also said: "They are all the same."[62]

---

[62] Muslim, 3/1219.

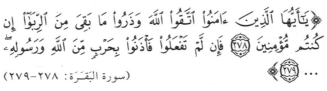

Based on this, it is not permitted to do work that involves writing interest-based contracts and conditions, paying or receiving *ribā*, depositing or guarding it. Generally speaking, it is *ḥarām* to be directly or indirectly involved with *ribā* in any way, shape or form.

The Prophet (ﷺ) was keen to explain the ugliness of this major sin. 'Abdullah ibn Mas'ood reported that the Prophet (ﷺ) said:

> "There are seventy-three types of *ribā*, the least of which is as abhorrent as a man having intercourse with his own mother."[63]

'Abdullah ibn Ḥan<u>dh</u>alah (رضي الله عنه) reported that the Prophet (ﷺ) said:

> "Knowingly consuming a dirham of *ribā* is worse for a man than committing adultery thirty-six times."[64]

The prohibition on *ribā* does not just apply to deals between rich and poor, as some people think; it is a general prohibition that applies to every person and every situation. How many rich people and big businessmen have gone bankrupt because of *ribā*! The least harm *ribā* does is to destroy the blessing (*barakah*) of the money, even if a person's wealth is great. The Prophet (ﷺ) said:

> "Even if *ribā* is much, it will end up being a small amount."[65]

---

[63] Al-Ḥākim, *al-Mustadrak*, 2/37; see also *Ṣaḥeeḥ al-Jāmi'*, hadith no. 3533.
[64] Aḥmad, 5/225; see also *Ṣaḥeeḥ al-Jāmi'*, hadith no. 3375.
[65] Al-Ḥākim, 2/37; see also *Ṣaḥeeḥ al-Jāmi'*, hadith no. 3542.

This does not refer to whether the ratio of interest is high or low; all *ribā* is *ḥarām*, and the one who deals with it will be raised up on the Day of Resurrection like the one who stands beaten by satan resulting in insanity and epilepsy.

In spite of the enormity of this sin, Allah has told us to repent of it and has explained how. Allah (ﷻ) says to those who deal with *ribā*:

﴿... وَإِن تُبْتُمْ فَلَكُمْ رُءُوسُ أَمْوَٰلِكُمْ لَا تَظْلِمُونَ وَلَا تُظْلَمُونَ ﴿٢٧٩﴾﴾ (سورة البَقـَرَة: ٢٧٩)

﴿... but if you repent, you shall have your capital sums. Deal not unjustly [by asking more than your capital sums], and you shall not be dealt with unjustly [by receiving less than your capital sums].﴾

(Qur'an 2: 279)

This is quintessential justice.

The believer must despise this major sin and feel its abhorrence, even if he puts his money in interest-based banks because he has no other choice and is afraid that his money may be lost or stolen. He should feel that he is compelled by necessity to do this, like one who eats dead meat, or worse. At the same time, he should seek the forgiveness of Allah and try to find an alternative if he can. He is not permitted to ask the bank for interest, and if the bank deposits it in his account, he must get rid of it in whatever way is permissible. This money cannot be counted as *ṣadaqah* (charity), because Allah (ﷻ) is pure and accepts only that which is pure. He cannot benefit from this money by using it to buy food, drink, clothing, transportation or housing; he cannot use it to fulfil obligations such as spending on his wife, children or parents, or to pay *zakāh* (poor-due) or taxes, or to defend himself in court. Rather, he should just get rid of it, for fear of the wrath of Allah.

29. Concealing product faults at the time of sale

The Prophet (ﷺ) once passed by a pile of food that was for sale. He put his hand in it and felt dampness, so he asked,

> "What is this, O' seller of the food?" He said, "It was rained on, O' Messenger of Allah." The Prophet said: "Why don't you put it on top, so that people can see it? Whoever deceives (people) is not one of us."[66]

There are many traders nowadays who do not fear Allah (ﷻ), and try to conceal faults by wrapping them in plastic, putting faulty produce in the bottom of the box, using chemicals and the like to make a product look good, or concealing noises in engines that may indicate a fault — so that when the purchaser brings a product home, it soon starts to wear out. Some traders change expiry dates, or prevent the buyer from examining or trying out a product. Many of those who sell cars or other types of equipment do not point out the product faults. All of this is *ḥarām*, as the Prophet (ﷺ) said:

> "The Muslim is the brother of his fellow Muslim. The Muslim is not permitted to sell to his brother anything which is faulty without pointing out the faults to him."[67]

---

[66] Muslim, 1/99.

[67] Ibn Mājah, 2/754; see also *Ṣaḥeeḥ al-Jāmi'*, hadith no. 6705.

Some traders even think that their responsibility ends when they tell buyers at an auction, "I am selling a heap of metal, a heap of metal..." This is a sale in which there is no blessing, as the Prophet (ﷺ) said:

> "The two parties involved in a sale have the choice (to end it) until they part. If both have been truthful and honest about any faults, the sale will be blessed, but if they have lied and concealed any faults, the sale will be unblessed."[68]

30. Artificially inflating prices

This refers to the practice of artificially inflating the price with no intention of buying, in order to deceive others, thus pushing them to add more to the price they are offering. The Prophet (ﷺ) said:

> "Do not artificially inflate prices."[69]

This is undoubtedly a form of deceit, and the Prophet (ﷺ) said:

> "Double-dealing and cheating will end in Hell."[70]

Many salesmen at auctions and in car salesrooms are earning unclean and *ḥarām* income because of the many *ḥarām* things they do, such as conspiring to artificially inflate prices and deceive purchasers, or to lower the price of one of their products, or conversely pretending to be customers and raising the prices at auctions to deceive and cheat.

---

[68] Bukhāri; see *Fatḥ al-Bāri*, 4/328.

[69] Ibid, 10/484.

[70] *Silsilat al-aḥādeeth aṣ-Ṣaḥeeḥah*, hadith no. 1057.

31. Trading after the second call to prayer on Friday

Allah (ﷻ) says:

﴿يَٰٓأَيُّهَا ٱلَّذِينَ ءَامَنُوٓا۟ إِذَا نُودِىَ لِلصَّلَوٰةِ مِن يَوْمِ ٱلْجُمُعَةِ فَٱسْعَوْا۟ إِلَىٰ ذِكْرِ ٱللَّهِ وَذَرُوا۟ ٱلْبَيْعَ ۚ ذَٰلِكُمْ خَيْرٌ لَّكُمْ إِن كُنتُمْ تَعْلَمُونَ ﴿٩﴾﴾ (سورة الجمعة: ٩)

﴿O' you who believe [Muslims]! When the call is proclaimed for the *Ṣalāh* [prayer] on the day of Friday [*Jumu'ah* prayer], come to the remembrance of Allah and leave off business [and every other thing]. That is better for you if you did know!﴾

(Qur'an 62: 9)

Some people continue trading in their stores and in front of the mosque even after the second call to prayer; those who buy from them also share in their guilt, even if they only buy a *siwāk* (natural toothbrush from an Arāk tree). According to the soundest opinion, this sale is invalid. Some owners of restaurants, bakeries and factories force their employees to work at the time of *Jumu'ah* prayers; even if this leads to an apparent increase in earnings, they will ultimately be losers in reality. The employee is obliged to act in accordance with the teaching of the Prophet (ﷺ):

> "There is no obedience to a created being if it involves disobedience to Allah."[71]

---

[71] Aḥmad, 1/129; Aḥmad Shākir said its *isnad* (attribution to a chain of narrators) is *ṣaḥeeḥ*, hadith no. 1065, also Bukhāri and Muslim.

32. Gambling

Allah (سُبْحَانَهُ وَتَعَالَىٰ) says:

﴿يَٰٓأَيُّهَا ٱلَّذِينَ ءَامَنُوٓاْ إِنَّمَا ٱلۡخَمۡرُ وَٱلۡمَيۡسِرُ وَٱلۡأَنصَابُ وَٱلۡأَزۡلَٰمُ رِجۡسٞ مِّنۡ عَمَلِ ٱلشَّيۡطَٰنِ فَٱجۡتَنِبُوهُ لَعَلَّكُمۡ تُفۡلِحُونَ ٩٠﴾ (سورة المائدة: ٩٠)

﴿O' you who believe! Intoxicants [all kinds of alcoholic drinks], gambling, *al-Anṣāb*, and *al-Azlām* [arrows for seeking luck or decision] are an abomination from satan's handiwork. So, [strictly] avoid it [abomination], in order that you may be successful.﴾ *(Qur'an 5: 90)*

Gambling was very common during the *Jāhiliyyah*; in one of the most well-known forms of gambling, ten people would buy a camel, each paying an equal share, then they would throw down arrows — a form of drawing lots. Seven people would win unequal shares and three would be left empty-handed.

Nowadays, there are many forms of gambling, including lotteries and raffles, in which people pay money to buy numbers, then numbers are drawn for first prize, second prize, and so on for a variety of prizes. This is *ḥarām*, even when it is supposedly done for charity.

Therefore, buying a product which includes something unknown or paying for a number for a draw which will decide who gets what is *ḥarām*.

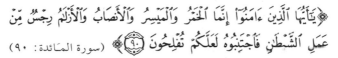

Another modern form of gambling is insurance, such as life insurance, car insurance, product insurance, insurance against fire or theft, third party insurance, comprehensive insurance, and so on. There are so many types of insurance that some singers even insure their voices!

All of the above are forms of gambling. Nowadays, there are even clubs that are devoted exclusively to gambling, in which there are the so-called "green tables" (roulette tables) just for people to commit this sin. Other forms of gambling include betting on horse races and other sports, fruit-machines and the like in amusement centres and competitions in which the victors win prizes, as a group of scholars have stated.

There are three kinds of competitive sports:

1. *Sharee'ah*-desired sports. It may be with or without prizes for the winners such as camel and horse race, shooting, marksmanship, javelin, science competition, Qur'an memorization etc.

2. Common legitimate sports such as Football matches, swimming competitions, taking care that they do not cause loss of obligatory prayers or cause of nakedness from Islamic point of view.

3. Competitions that are *ḥarām* in themselves or lead to *ḥarām*, such as beauty competitions, boxing aimed at face, bull/ram fighting, cock fighting etc.

33. Theft

Allah (سُبْحَانَهُ وَتَعَالَى) says:

﴿وَٱلسَّارِقُ وَٱلسَّارِقَةُ فَٱقْطَعُوٓا۟ أَيْدِيَهُمَا جَزَآءًۢ بِمَا كَسَبَا نَكَٰلًا مِّنَ ٱللَّهِ ۗ وَٱللَّهُ عَزِيزٌ حَكِيمٌ ﴿٣٨﴾﴾ (سورة المائدة: ٣٨)

﴾And [as for] the male thief and the female thief, cut off [from the wrist joint] their [right] hands as a recompense for that which they committed, a punishment by way of example from Allah. And Allah is All-Powerful, All-Wise.﴿ *(Qur'an 5: 38)*

One of the worst forms of this sin is stealing from the pilgrims who come on *Ḥajj* and *'Umrah* to the Ancient House of Allah. This kind of thief has no respect for the limits set by Allah in the best region on earth and around the House of Allah. In the report about *Ṣalāt al-Kusoof* (the eclipse prayer), it is reported that the Prophet (ﷺ) said:

"Hell was brought near, and that was when you saw me stepping backwards, because I feared that its heat would touch me. I saw therein a man with a crooked stick dragging his intestines in the Fire. He used to steal from the *Ḥujjāj* (pilgrims) with his crooked stick. If they spotted him, he would say, 'This got caught on my stick,' and if they did not spot him, he would take whatever he had stolen..."[72]

Another one of the worst forms of theft is stealing from the public purse — treasury. Some of those who do this say: "We are only doing what others do." They do not realize that what they are doing is effectively stealing from all Muslims, because the public purse belongs to all Muslims. Imitating those who do not fear Allah is no excuse. Some people steal from the wealth of the *kuffār* (disbelievers) on the grounds that they are *kuffār*, but this is wrong; the only *kuffār* whose wealth we are allowed to take away

---

[72] Muslim, hadith no. 904.

are those who are actively fighting Muslims (in the battlefield), which does not apply to every *kāfir*, individual or company.

Another form of theft is pick-pocketing, stealing something from a person's pocket without him realizing. Some thieves enter people's houses as visitors, and steal from them. Some steal from their guests' bags. Some — including women — go into stores and hide things in their pockets or under their clothing. Some think that the theft of small or cheap items is of little consequence, but the Prophet (ﷺ) said:

> "Allah has cursed the thief who steals an egg and has his hand cut off, and the thief who steals a rope and has his hand cut off."[73]

Everyone who steals something must first repent to Allah (ﷻ), then return the item to its rightful owner, whether openly or secretly, in person or via a third party. If he fails to find the rightful owner or his heirs after much effort, then he should give the property in charity, with the intention that the reward should be given to the rightful owner.

34. Offering or accepting bribes

Giving a bribe to a *qāḍi* (judge) to make him turn a blind eye to the truth or to make a false claim succeed is a sin, because it leads to oppression and injustice for the person who is in the right, and it spreads corruption. Allah (ﷻ) says:

---

[73] Bukhāri, see *Fatḥ al-Bāri*, 12/81.

﴿وَلَا تَأْكُلُوٓا۟ أَمْوَٰلَكُم بَيْنَكُم بِٱلْبَٰطِلِ وَتُدْلُوا۟ بِهَآ إِلَى ٱلْحُكَّامِ لِتَأْكُلُوا۟ فَرِيقًا مِّنْ أَمْوَٰلِ ٱلنَّاسِ بِٱلْإِثْمِ وَأَنتُمْ تَعْلَمُونَ ﴿١٨٨﴾﴾

(سورة البَقَـرَة: ١٨٨)

﴾And eat up not one another's property unjustly, not give bribery to the rulers [judges before presenting your cases] that you may knowingly eat up a part of the property of others sinfully.﴿ *(Qur'an 2: 188)*

Abu Hurayrah (ﷺ) reported that the Prophet (ﷺ) said:

"Allah has cursed those who give and accept bribes with regard to (any) judgement."[74]

However, payments made in order to reach the truth or avert injustice when there is no other way of doing so are not included in this warning.

Bribery is so widespread nowadays that it is more of a source of income than the regular salary for some workers. Some companies even include bribes as a factor in their budgets, under a variety of headings, and some dealings cannot begin or end without the payment of a bribe. Much harm is caused to the poor and many safeguards are broken because of bribes. Bribery is a cause of corruption whereby employees act against their employers, and one can only get good service if he pays a bribe — the person who refuses to pay will get shoddy or late service, and people who come after him but are willing to pay will be served before him. Because of bribery, a great deal of money which is due to employers ends up in the pockets of sales representatives and those responsible for making company purchases. It is little

---

[74] Aḥmad, 2/387; see also *Ṣaḥeeḥ al-Jāmi'*, hadith no. 5069.

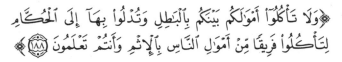

wonder, then, that the Prophet (ﷺ) prayed to Allah to deprive all those involved of His Mercy. 'Abdullah ibn 'Amr (رضي الله عنه) reported that the Messenger of Allah (ﷺ) said:

> "The curse of Allah be upon the one who gives a bribe and the one who accepts it."[75]

35. Seizing land by force

When there is no fear of Allah (سبحانه وتعالى), strength and cunning are a disaster because the one who possesses these qualities uses them to oppress others, such as seizing other people's possessions, including their land. The punishment for this is extremely severe. 'Abdullah ibn 'Umar (رضي الله عنه) reported that the Prophet (ﷺ) said:

> "Whoever seizes any piece of land unlawfully, Allah will make the ground swallow him up to the seventh depth of the earth on the Day of Resurrection."[76]

Ya'lā ibn Murrah (رضي الله عنه) reported that the Prophet (ﷺ) said:

> "Any man who seizes a hand-span of land, Allah will tell him to dig it (according to aṭ-Ṭabarāni: to bring it) to the seventh depth of the earth, then it will be placed around his neck on the Day of Resurrection, until Allah has finished judging mankind."[77]

This also includes changing landmarks and boundaries in order to make one's own land bigger at the expense of a neighbour, as is indicated by the words of the Prophet (ﷺ):

---

[75] Ibn Mājah, hadith no. 2313; see also *Ṣaḥeeḥ al-Jāmi'*, hadith no. 5114.

[76] Bukhāri; see *Fatḥ al-Bāri* 5/103.

[77] Aṭ-Ṭabarāni in *al-Kabeer*, 22/270; see also *Ṣaḥeeḥ al-Jāmi'*, hadith no. 2719.

"Allah has cursed the one who changes the boundary-markers of the land."[78]

36. Accepting gift/s for interceding

To have a position of high standing among people is one of the blessings of Allah (ﷻ) to His slave, if he is grateful. One way in which a person may give thanks for this blessing is by using his position to benefit other Muslims. This is part of the general meaning of the hadith:

"Whoever among you is able to benefit his brother, then let him do so."[79]

The person who uses his position to benefit others by averting injustice or bringing some good, without doing anything that is *ḥarām* or infringes on the rights of others, will be rewarded by Allah (ﷻ), so long as his intention is sincere, as the Prophet (ﷺ) told us:

"Intercede, you will be rewarded."[80]

It is not permitted to accept anything in return for this intercession or mediation. Evidence for this may be seen in the hadith narrated by Abu Umāmah (رضي الله عنه):

"Whoever intercedes for someone then accepts a gift (in return for it), enters the great door among the doors of *ribā*."[81]

---

[78] Muslim, with commentary by an-Nawawi, 13/141.

[79] Muslim, 4/1726.

[80] Abu Dāwood, 5132; also reported in Bukhāri and Muslim, see *Fatḥ al-Bāri*, 10/450, *Kitāb al-adab, Bāb ta'āwun al-mu'mineen ba'ḍuhum ba'ḍan.*

[81] Aḥmad, 5/261; see *Ṣaḥeeḥ al-Jāmi'*, hadith no. 6292.

Some people offer the opportunity to benefit from their position, in return for a sum of money, in order to help someone get a job, or a transfer from one office or area to another, or treatment for the sick, etc. The soundest opinion is that this exchange is *ḥarām*, because of the hadith of Abu Umāmah quoted above, whose apparent meaning is that accepting such gifts is wrong, even if no agreement was previously made.[82]

The reward which the doer of good will receive from Allah (ﷻ) on the Day of Judgement should be sufficient. A man came to al-Ḥasan ibn Sahl asking him to intercede for him in some matter, which he did; then the man came to thank him. Al-Ḥasan ibn Sahl said to him, "Why are you thanking us? We believe that zakāh is due on positions of rank just as it is due on wealth."[83]

It is worth pointing out here that there is a difference between hiring someone to do legal paperwork for you and paying him wages in return, which has to do with the legitimate hiring of labour, and using a person's position to intercede for you in return for money, which is *ḥarām*.

37. Hiring someone and benefitting by his labour, then not paying him his wages

The Prophet (ﷺ) encouraged speedy payment of wages to people hired for their labour. He (ﷺ) said:

> "Give the hired man his wages before his sweat dries."[84]

---

[82] From the verbal statements of Imam 'Abdul-'Aziz ibn Bāz.

[83] Ibn Mufliḥ, *al-Ādāb ash-Shar'iyyah*, 2/176.

[84] Ibn Mājah, 2/817; see also *Ṣaḥeeḥ al-Jāmi'*, hadith no. 1493.

One form of oppression or injustice that is common in Muslim societies is the failure to give employees and workers their rights. This takes many forms, for example:

— Denying an employee's rights in totality, where the employee has no proof of his rights. He may have lost his dues in this world, but he will not lose them before Allah (ﷻ) on the Day of Resurrection. So, the oppressor who consumed the money due to the victim will be brought forth, and his victim will be given some of his *ḥasanāt* (good deeds) in compensation (i.e. some of the oppressor's good deeds will be added to his victim's credit). If the *ḥasanāt* are not enough, some of the victim's *sayyi'āt* (bad deeds) will be added to the oppressor, then he will be thrown into Hell.

— Not giving the employee his full rights. Allah (ﷻ) says:

﴿وَيْلٌ لِّلْمُطَفِّفِينَ ۝١﴾ (سورة المطفّفين: ١)

﴿Woe to *al-Muṭaffifeen* [those who give less in measure and weight (decrease the rights of others)].﴾ *(Qur'an 83: 1)*

One example of this is the action of a boss who brings workers from their homelands with a contract to pay a certain wage. Once the people are committed and have started to work for him, he goes and changes the contracts, altering them to state a lower wage than the one actually agreed upon. The employees stay because they have no choice and have no proof of their rights; all they can do is complain to Allah (ﷻ). If the employer is a Muslim and the employee is not, this lowering of wages is a way of turning people away from the Straight Path, and he [the employer] will carry his [the employee's] sin.

— Also making the employee do extra work or put in longer hours, without paying him overtime or giving him any more than the basic salary.

— Some bosses delay payment of wages and pay up only after much struggle, complaining, chasing and court cases. Their aim may be to make the employee give up his claim to his rightful wages and stop asking; or they may want to invest this money, perhaps by lending it for interest. Meanwhile, the poor employee cannot buy his daily bread or send anything home to his needy wife and children for whose sake he left to work overseas. Woe to those oppressors on that painful Day! Abu Hurayrah (رضي الله عنه) reported that the Prophet (ﷺ) said:

> "Allah says: 'There are three whom I will oppose on the Day of Resurrection: a man who gives his word swearing by Me then breaks it, a man who sells a free man into slavery and keeps the money, and a man who hires another and benefits from his labour then does not pay him his wages.'"[85]

38. Not giving gifts equally to one's children

Some people show favouritism in the way they give gifts to some of their children but not to others. According to the soundest opinion, doing this is *ḥarām* unless there is some legitimate reason, such as one child being in greater need than the others due to sickness, being in debt, being rewarded for having memorized the entire Qur'an, being unable to find a job, having a large family, being a full-time student, etc. When a father gives

[85] Bukhāri, see *Fatḥ al-Bāri*, 4/447.

something to one of his children who is in need, he should have the intention to give similarly to any other children of his, should the need arise. General proof of this principle may be seen in the *āyah*:

﴿... ٱعْدِلُوا۟ هُوَ أَقْرَبُ لِلتَّقْوَىٰ ۖ وَٱتَّقُوا۟ ٱللَّهَ ... ﴿٨﴾﴾

(سورة المائدة: ٨)

﴿... Be just: that is nearer to piety; and fear Allah...﴾
(Qur'an 5: 8)

Specific evidence is found in the report of an-Nu'mān ibn Basheer (رضي الله عنه), whose father brought him to the Messenger of Allah (ﷺ) and said:

> "I have given this son of mine a slave that I had." The Messenger of Allah asked him, "Did you give all your children a similar gift?" He said, "No." The Prophet said: "Then take it (the gift) back."[86]

According to another report, the Prophet (ﷺ) said:

> "Fear Allah and be fair to your children," so he went away and took his gift back.[87]

According to a third report, he (ﷺ) said,

> "Do not ask me to be a witness, for I will not bear witness to injustice."[88]

---

[86] Bukhāri, see *Fatḥ al-Bāri*, 5/211.

[87] Ibid.

[88] Muslim, 3/1243.

Sons may be given twice as much as daughters, as in the case of inheritance, according to Imam Aḥmad, may Allah have mercy on him.[89]

There are some families where fathers do not fear Allah (ﷻ), and their favouritism creates hatred and jealousy among the children. A father may give one child more because he looks like his paternal uncles, and may give less to another child because he looks like his maternal uncles; or he may give more to the children of one wife and less to the children of another wife; or he may put one wife's children in private schools, but not the other wife's children. This will ultimately backfire on him, because, in most cases, the one who is deprived in this way will not respect his father or treat him kindly in the future. The Prophet (ﷺ) asked the man who showed favouritism to one son,

> "Do you not want all your children to respect you equally?"[90]

39. Asking people for money when one is not in need

Sahl ibn al-Ḥandhaliyyah (رضي الله عنه) reported that the Messenger of Allah (ﷺ) said:

> "Whoever asks people for money when he has what is sufficient for him is only asking for more of the embers of Hell." They asked him, "O' Messenger of Allah! What is sufficient so that he does not have to

[89] Abu Dāwood, *Masā'il al-Imam Aḥmad*, 204; Imam Ibn al-Qayyim explained this in more detail in his footnotes.

[90] Aḥmad, 4/269; see also *Ṣaḥeeḥ al-Jāmi'*, hadith no. 1623.

> ask for more?" He said: "Having enough to eat lunch and dinner."[91]

Ibn Mas'ood (رضي الله عنه) reported that the Messenger of Allah, blessings and peace be upon him, said:

> "Whoever asks people for money when he has what is sufficient for him will come on the Day of Judgement with scratches and lacerations on his face."[92]

Some beggars come to mosques, interrupting people's worship with their complaints; some of them lie, bringing forged papers and telling tall stories; some of them distribute their family members around different mosques, then they regroup and move on to other mosques. Some of these people may in fact be well-off to an extent which only Allah (سبحانه وتعالى) knows; only when they die do others find out what they left behind. Meanwhile, there are others who are truly in need, but people are not aware of it and may think they have enough, because they are too proud and do not beg of people at all; nobody knows their true situation, so no one gives them charity.

40. Seeking a loan with the intention of not paying it back

The dues owed by one person to another are very important in the sight of Allah, so much so that if a person falls short in his duties towards Allah (سبحانه وتعالى), he may be forgiven if he repents, but when it comes to the rights of other people, he has to fulfil them

[91] Abu Dāwood, 2/281; see also *Ṣaḥeeḥ al-Jāmi'*, hadith no. 6280.

[92] Aḥmad, 1/388; see also *Ṣaḥeeḥ al-Jāmi'*, hadith no. 6255.

before the Day comes when dinars and dirhams will be of no avail, and only *ḥasanāt* and *sayyi'āt* (good and bad deeds) will count. Allah (ﷻ) says:

﴿ إِنَّ ٱللَّهَ يَأْمُرُكُمْ أَن تُؤَدُّوا۟ ٱلْأَمَـٰنَـٰتِ إِلَىٰٓ أَهْلِهَا ... ﴿٥٨﴾ ﴾

(سورة النّسَاء: ٥٨)

﴿Verily! Allah commands that you should render back the trusts to their owners...﴾ *(Qur'an 4: 58)*

One of the widespread problems in our society is this casual approach to loans; some people take out loans not for some urgent need but because they want to expand their businesses or keep up with others by buying new cars, furniture or other temporary luxuries of this life. Often these people let themselves in for the confusion of installment plans, which are dubious or maybe even *ḥarām*.

A casual approach to loans leads people to delay repayments, which in turn leads to loss and financial ruin of others. Warning of the consequences of this deed, the Prophet (ﷺ) said:

> "Whoever takes people's money with the intention of paying them back, Allah will pay him back, but whoever takes people's money with the intention of wasting it, Allah will destroy him."[93]

People take the matter of loans very lightly, but in the sight of Allah (ﷻ) it is a serious matter, so much so that even the *shaheed* (martyr), with his immense reward and high status, is not

---

[93] Bukhāri; see *Fatḥ al-Bāri*, 5/54.

free of the consequences of debt. Evidence of this is seen in the hadith:

> "Glory be to Allah, Who has revealed the seriousness of debt. By the One in Whose hand is my soul, if a man were slain in the way of Allah, then brought back to life, then killed again and brought back to life again, then killed a third time, but he owed a debt, he would not be admitted to Paradise until his debt was paid off."[94]

Now, will these squanderers be deterred from such a casual approach?

41. Consuming *ḥarām* wealth

The person who does not fear Allah (ﷻ) does not care where from he earns his money or how he spends it; his only concern is to increase his bank balance, even if it is *ḥarām* and ill-gotten by means of theft, bribery, extortion, forgery, selling *ḥarām* things, *ribā* (usury), consuming an orphan's wealth, earning from *ḥarām* work like fortune-telling, immorality or singing, stealing from the Muslim treasury or public property, taking people's money by coercion or high-pressure sales tactics, begging when one is not in need, etc. Then he buys food, clothing and transportation with this ill-gotten money, builds or rents a house, furnishes it and fills his stomach with *ḥarām* food. The Prophet (ﷺ) said:

---

[94] An-Nasā'i; see *al-Mujtabā*, 7/314, and *Ṣaḥeeḥ al-Jāmi'*, hadith no. 3594.

"Any flesh that grows from ill-gotten gains is more deserving of being touched by Hell-fire..."[95]

On the Day of Resurrection, each person will be asked how he earned money and on what he spent it, and there will be doom and loss. Anyone who still has *ḥarām* money should hasten to get rid of it; if it is due to anyone else, then he should hasten to return it and ask for his forgiveness before there comes a Day on which dinars and dirhams will be of no avail, when only *ḥasanāt* and *sayyi'āt* will count.

42. Drinking *khamr* (Alcohol), even a single drop

Allah, the All-High, says:

﴿... إِنَّمَا ٱلْخَمْرُ وَٱلْمَيْسِرُ وَٱلْأَنصَابُ وَٱلْأَزْلَٰمُ رِجْسٌ مِّنْ عَمَلِ ٱلشَّيْطَٰنِ فَٱجْتَنِبُوهُ لَعَلَّكُمْ تُفْلِحُونَ ﴿٩٠﴾﴾ (سورة المائدة: ٩٠)

﴿... Intoxicants [all kinds of alcoholic drinks], and gambling, *al-Anṣāb* [stone altars for sacrifices to idols, etc.] and *al-Azlām* [arrows for seeking luck or decision] are an abomination of satan's handi-work. So avoid it [strictly] that you may be successful.﴾ *(Qur'an 5: 90)*

The command to avoid these things is the strongest indication that they are forbidden. *Khamr* (wine, alcohol) is compared to *al-Anṣāb*, which were idols of the *kuffār*; there is no excuse for those who argue that the Qur'an does not say it is forbidden but only tells us to avoid it!

---

[95] Aṭ-Ṭabarāni: *al-Kabeer*, 19/136; see also *Ṣaḥeeḥ al-Jāmi'*, hadith no. 4495.

The Prophet (ﷺ) also issued a stern warning to the one who drinks *khamr*. Jābir (رضي الله عنه) reported that he (ﷺ) said:

> "Allah has promised the one who drinks *khamr* that He will make him drink the mud of *khibāl*." The people asked, "O' Messenger of Allah! What is the mud of *khibāl*?" He said, "The sweat of the people of Hell, or the juice of the people of Hell."[96]

Ibn 'Abbās (رضي الله عنه) reported that the Prophet (ﷺ) said:

> "Whoever dies with the habit of drinking *khamr* will meet Allah as one who worships idols."[97]

Nowadays, there are so many kinds of *khamr*, with many names in Arabic and other languages, such as, *ji'ah* (beer), alcohol, *araq* ("arrack"), vodka, champagne, etc. There has appeared in this *ummah* the type of person described by the Prophet (ﷺ):

> "Some people of my *ummah* will drink *khamr*, calling it by another name."[98]

So they may call it "spirits" instead of *khamr*, as an attempt to distort the facts and deceive. Allah (سبحانه وتعالى) says:

﴿يُخَـٰدِعُونَ ٱللَّهَ وَٱلَّذِينَ ءَامَنُوا۟ وَمَا يَخْدَعُونَ إِلَّآ أَنفُسَهُمْ وَمَا يَشْعُرُونَ ﴿٩﴾﴾ (سورة البقرة: ٩)

---

[96] Muslim, 3/1587.

[97] Aṭ-Ṭabarāni, 12/45; see also *Ṣaḥeeḥ al-Jāmi'*, hadith no. 6525.

[98] Aḥmad, 5/342; see also *Ṣaḥeeḥ al-Jāmi'*, hadith no. 5453.

> ﴾They [think they] deceive Allah and those who believe, while they only deceive themselves, and perceive [it] not!﴿ *(Qur'an 2: 9)*

Islam imposes strict control on this matter, and deals with it decisively so that there is no room for misunderstanding. The Prophet (ﷺ) said:

> "Every intoxicant is *khamr* and every intoxicant is *ḥarām*."[99]

Everything that has the effect of clouding the mind is *ḥarām*, whether in large or small amounts. The hadith says,

> "Whatever causes intoxication in large amounts, a small amount of it is *ḥarām*."[100]

No matter how many different names there are, they all refer to one thing, and the ruling concerning it is well-known.

Finally, the Prophet issued a warning to those who take *khamr*:

> "Whoever takes *khamr* and becomes intoxicated, his prayers will not be accepted for forty days, and if he dies he will enter Hell, and if he repents Allah will accept his repentance. If he drinks again and becomes intoxicated again, his prayers will not be accepted for forty days, and if he dies he will enter Hell, and if he repents Allah will accept his repentance. If he drinks again and becomes intoxicated again, his prayers will not be accepted for forty days, and if he dies he will enter Hell, and if he repents Allah will accept his

---

[99] Muslim, 3/1587.

[100] Abu Dāwood, hadith no. 3681; see *Ṣaḥeeḥ Abu Dāwood*, hadith no. 3128.

repentance. If he drinks a fourth time, Allah promises that He will make him drink from the mud of *khibāl* on the Day of Resurrection. The people asked, 'O' Messenger of Allah! What is the mud of *khibāl*?' He said, 'The juice of the burning people of Hell.' "[101]

43. Using vessels of gold and silver, or eating and drinking from them

Nowadays, hardly any stores of household goods are free of vessels made of gold and silver, or plated with these metals. The same applies to homes of rich people and many hotels. This kind of thing has become one of the precious gifts that people give one another on special occasions. Some people may not have these things at home, but they use them in other people's homes when invited to a meal. All of these are actions which are forbidden in Islam. The Prophet (ﷺ) issued a stern warning about using such vessels. Umm Salamah reported that he (ﷺ) said:

> "The one who eats or drinks from a vessel of gold or silver is putting fire from Hell into his stomach."[102]

This ruling applies to every kind of vessel or utensil made of gold or silver, such as plates, forks, spoons, knives, trays on which food is served, boxes of sweets which are given to wedding guests and so on. Some people might say,

> "We are not using them, we are just putting them on display in a glass case."

---

101 Ibn Mājah, hadith no. 3377; see also *Ṣaḥeeḥ al-Jāmi'*, hadith no. 6313.

102 Muslim, 3/1634.

This is not permitted either, to prevent any possibility of these things being used.[103]

44. Bearing false witness

Allah (ﷻ) says:

﴿... فَٱجْتَنِبُوا۟ ٱلرِّجْسَ مِنَ ٱلْأَوْثَـٰنِ وَٱجْتَنِبُوا۟ قَوْلَ ٱلزُّورِ ۝٣٠ حُنَفَآءَ لِلَّهِ غَيْرَ مُشْرِكِينَ بِهِۦ ... ۝٣١﴾

(سورة الحجّ: ٣٠-٣١)

﴾... So shun the abomination of [worshipping] idols, and shun lying speech [false statements] — *Ḥunafā' Lillah* [i.e. worshiping none but Allah], not associating partners [in worship, etc.] unto Him...﴿ *(Qur'an 22: 30-31)*

'Abdur-Raḥmān ibn Abu Bakrah (may Allah be pleased with him and his father), reported that his father narrated, "We were with the Messenger of Allah when he said:

> 'Should I not warn you about three major sins' — he repeated it three times, then said: 'associating partners with Allah, disobedience to parents, and... ' — he was reclining but he sat up at this point and said — 'and bearing false witness.' He kept repeating this with such fervour that we wished he would stop."[104]

The warning against bearing false witness was uttered repeatedly because people take it too lightly and there are many

---

[103] From the oral statements of Sheikh 'Abdul-'Azeez ibn Bāz.

[104] Bukhāri, see *Fatḥ al-Bāri*, 5/261.

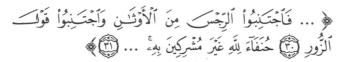

motives for doing so, such as hatred and envy. The resulting corruption is great indeed. How many people have lost their rights because of false witness! How many innocent people have been treated unjustly, and how many people have gained what they did not deserve, because of it!

An example of the ways in which people take this matter lightly is what sometimes happens in the courts, when a person might say to someone he has only just met, "Testify for me and I will testify for you." So one might testify for the other in a case where he does not have the necessary knowledge of what really happened, like testifying that this person owns a piece of land or a house, or recommending him when he has never seen him before that day in court. This is lying and false witness, whereas testimony should be as described in the Book of Allah (ﷻ):

﴿... وَمَا شَهِدْنَآ إِلَّا بِمَا عَلِمْنَا ... ﴾ (٨١)

(سورة يُوسُف: ٨١)

﴾... we did not testify except to what we knew,...﴿ *(Qur'an 12: 81)*

45. Listening to music and musical instruments

Ibn Mas'ood (رضي الله عنه) used to swear by Allah (ﷻ) that the *āyah*:

﴿وَمِنَ ٱلنَّاسِ مَن يَشْتَرِى لَهْوَ ٱلْحَدِيثِ لِيُضِلَّ عَن سَبِيلِ ٱللَّهِ ... ﴾ (٦)

(سورة لقمَان: ٦)

﴾And of mankind is he who purchases idle talk [i.e. music, singing, etc.] to mislead [men] from the Path of Allah...﴿ *(Qur'an 31: 6)* referred to singing[105], Abu ʻĀmir and Abu Mālik al-Ashʻari (ﷺ) reported that the Prophet (ﷺ) said:

> "Among my *ummah* will be people who will make permissible *al-ḥerra, al-ḥareer, al-khamr* and *al-maʻāzif* — liberalism, silk, alcohol and musical instruments..."[106]

Anas (ﷺ) reported that the Prophet (ﷺ) said:

> "In this *ummah*, there will be punishments of earth-quakes, showers of stones and deformity (transform-ation into animals); when the people will be involved in drinking *khamr* (intoxicants), listen to female singers and play musical instruments."[107]

The Prophet (ﷺ) forbade the "*koobah*" (a kind of drum), and described the flute as the voice of the immoral fool. The early scholars such as Imam Aḥmad, (may Allah have mercy on him), stated that musical instruments such as the *'ood* (lute), *ṭanboor* (a long-necked stringed instrument), reed flute, *rabāb* (rebec) (stringed instrument resembling a fiddle) and cymbal, are *ḥarām*. There is no doubt that modern instruments such as the violin, *qānoon* (stringed musical instrument resembling a zither), organ, piano, guitar, etc., are also included in the Prophet's prohibition of musical instruments, because their effect and impact is greater than that of the ancient instruments mentioned in some hadiths. They are even more intoxicating than *khamr*, as scholars such as

---

[105] *Tafseer ibn Katheer*, 6/333.

[106] Bukhāri; see *Fatḥ al-Bāri*, 10/51.

[107] *Silsilat al-aḥādeeth aṣ-Ṣaheeḥah*, hadith no. 2203; attributed to Ibn Abi Dunyā, concerning *Dhamm al-Malāhi* (condemnation of musical instruments); the hadith is narrated by At-Tirmidhi, hadith no. 2212.

Ibn al-Qayyim mentioned. Hence, the prohibition and the sin involved are greater when the music is accompanied by singing in the voices of female singers, and it is even worse when the lyrics speak of love and describe physical beauty. Some scholars said that singing paves the way for *zinā* (adultery or fornication), and that it makes hypocrisy grow in the heart. Generally speaking, music and singing form one of the greatest temptations of our times.

What is very difficult is the fact that music is nowadays a part of so many things, such as clocks, doorbells, children's toys, computers, telephones, etc., and avoiding it takes a great deal of determination, in which Allah (سبحانه وتعالى) is the only source of help.

46. Gossiping and backbiting

Many gatherings produce nothing but gossip about other Muslims and slander of their honour. This is something which Allah (سبحانه وتعالى) has forbidden for His slaves, and has drawn the most repulsive analogy to put them off. He (سبحانه وتعالى) says:

﴿... وَلَا يَغْتَب بَّعْضُكُم بَعْضًا ۚ أَيُحِبُّ أَحَدُكُمْ أَن يَأْكُلَ
لَحْمَ أَخِيهِ مَيْتًا فَكَرِهْتُمُوهُ ۚ ... ﴿١٢﴾﴾ (سورة الحجرات: ١٢)

﴿...neither backbite one another. Would one of you like to eat the flesh of his brother when dead? You would hate it [so hate backbiting]...﴾

(Qur'an 49: 12)

The Prophet (ﷺ) explained the meaning of this *āyah*. He (ﷺ) said:

> "Do you know what *gheebah* (gossip or backbiting) is?" They said, "Allah and His Messenger know best." He said: "To say something about your brother, that he does not want to be said." He was asked, "What do you think if what is said about him is true?" He said, "If what you say about him is true, it is backbiting, and if what you say about him is not true, it is calumny."[108]

Gossiping or backbiting means saying something about a Muslim which may be true but which he does not like to hear spoken, whether it be about his physical appearance, his adherence to religion, his worldly affairs, his self, his behaviour or his character. There are many forms of gossip, including talking about a person's faults and imitating him to make fun of him.

People take the matter of *gheebah* very lightly, although it is very serious in the sight of Allah, as is indicated by the words of the Prophet (ﷺ):

> "There are seventy-two forms of *ribā*, the least of which is as bad as a man having intercourse with his own mother, and the worst of which is when a man slanders the honour of his brother."[109]

Whoever is present in a gathering where gossip takes place should "forbid what is evil" and defend his absent brother. The Prophet (ﷺ) encouraged us to do this when he said:

---

[108] Muslim, 4/2001.

[109] *Silsilat al-aḥādeeth aṣ-Ṣaheeḥah*, hadith no. 1871.

"Whoever defends the honour of his Muslim brother, Allah will protect his face from the Fire on the Day of Resurrection."[110]

47. Slandering

Some people go about repeating the words of others to cause trouble among them; this is one of the greatest causes of broken relations and stirring up feelings of hatred among people. Allah (ﷻ) condemned the one who does it,

﴿وَلَا تُطِعْ كُلَّ حَلَّافٍ مَّهِينٍ ﴿١٠﴾ هَمَّازٍ مَّشَّآءٍ بِنَمِيمٍ ﴿١١﴾﴾

(سورة القَلَم: ١٠-١١)

﴾And [O' Muhammad] obey you not every *Ḥallaf Maheen* [the one who swears much and is a liar or is worthless]. A slanderer, going about with calumnies.﴿ *(Qur'an 68: 10-11)*

Ḥudhayfah reported that the Prophet (ﷺ) said:

"No eavesdropper will enter Paradise."[111]

Ibn 'Abbās (رضي الله عنه) said: "The Prophet (ﷺ) passed by one of the gardens of Madeenah, and heard the sound of two people being punished in their graves. The Prophet (ﷺ) said:

"They are being punished, but they are not being punished for any major sin; one of them never used to

---

[110] Aḥmad, 6/450; see also *Ṣaḥeeḥ al-Jāmi'*, hadith no. 6238.

[111] Bukhāri, see *Fatḥ al-Bāri*, 10/472; *An-Nihāyah*: Ibn al-Atheer, 4/11. "Eavesdrop-per" here refers to a person who eavesdrops on others without their knowing, then goes and tells others what he has heard.

clean himself properly after urinating, and the other used to spread malicious slander..."[112]

One of the worst forms of this sin is to cause trouble between a husband and wife, or vice versa, or to tell one's boss what other employees are saying, in order to create trouble. All of this is *ḥarām*.

48. Looking into people's houses without their permission

Allah (ﷻ) says:

﴿يَٰٓأَيُّهَا ٱلَّذِينَ ءَامَنُوا۟ لَا تَدْخُلُوا۟ بُيُوتًا غَيْرَ بُيُوتِكُمْ حَتَّىٰ تَسْتَأْنِسُوا۟ وَتُسَلِّمُوا۟ عَلَىٰٓ أَهْلِهَا ... ﴿٢٧﴾﴾ (سورة النّور: ٢٧)

﴾O' you who believe! Enter not houses other than your own, until you have asked permission and greeted those in them;...﴿ *(Qur'an 24: 27)*

The Prophet (ﷺ) explained that the reason for seeking permission was the fear that the person entering the house might see something private .

"The rule of seeking permission has been established for the sake of (not) seeing (i.e., sighting unwanted scene)."[113]

Nowadays, when houses and buildings are too close to one another or even attached, and doors and windows face one another, the possibility of neighbours seeing one another has

---

[112] Bukhāri; see *Fatḥ al-Bāri*, 1/317.

[113] Ibid, 11/24.

increased greatly. Many people do not lower their gaze, and some of those who live on higher floors may deliberately look down from their roofs and windows into neighbouring homes that are lower than their own. This is an act of betrayal and an invasion of their neighbours' privacy, as well as being the way that leads to *ḥarām* deeds. A great deal of misery and trouble has resulted from this, and the fact that the *Sharee'ah* counts the eye of the one who spies as worthless is a sufficient proof of the seriousness of the matter. The Messenger of Allah (ﷺ) said:

> "Whoever looks into somebody's house without their permission, it is permissible for them to put out his eye."[114]

According to another report, he said:

> "Put out his eye, and there will be no penalty or retribution."[115]

49. Two persons conversing privately excluding a third

This is one of the problems that exist in social gatherings, and it is one of the ways in which satan divides the Muslims and makes some of them hate others. The Prophet (ﷺ) explained the rule and the wisdom behind it:

> "If you are three, then two should not converse privately to the exclusion of a third until you are joined by other people, because this will make him sad."[116]

---

[114] Muslim, 3/1699.

[115] Aḥmad, 2/385; see also *Ṣaḥeeḥ al-Jāmi'*, hadith no. 6022.

[116] Bukhāri, see *Fatḥ al-Bāri*, 11/83.

This also includes three people talking privately to the exclusion of a fourth, and so on, and two people speaking in a language which the third does not understand, because this is undoubtedly a form of disdain towards the third, which gives the impression that they intend to hurt him, etc.

50. *Isbāl* - Wearing clothes that come down below the ankles

One of the things which people treat as insignificant, although it is serious in the sight of Allah (ﷻ), is *isbāl*, which means lengthening one's clothes below the ankles; some people let their clothes touch the ground, and some allow them to drag on the floor behind them.

Abu Dharr (رضي الله عنه) reported that the Prophet (ﷺ) said:

> "There are three to whom Allah will not speak to on the Day of Resurrection, nor look at, nor purify: the one who wears his lower garment below the ankles; the one who reminds others of his gifts or favours; and the one who sells his product by means of lies and false oaths."[117]

The one who says "I am not wearing my clothes below my ankles out of arrogance" is in fact praising himself in a way that is unacceptable. The warning against *isbāl* is issued to all, regardless of whether they do it out of arrogance or not, as the Prophet (ﷺ) said:

[117] Muslim, 1/102.

> "Whatever part of the lower garment is below the ankles is in Hell."[118]

The person whose *isbāl* is the result of arrogance will be more severely punished than the one who has no such intention, as the Prophet (ﷺ) said:

> "Whoever trails his garment out of pride, Allah will not even look at him on the Day of Resurrection."[119]

Wearing any clothes below the ankle is *ḥarām*, as indicated in the hadith reported by Ibn 'Umar (رضي الله عنه):

> "*Isbāl* may be done with an *izār* (lower garment), *qameeṣ* (shirt or upper garment) and *'amāmah* (turban); whoever drags any part of them on the ground out of pride, Allah will not look at him on the Day of Resurrection."[120]

Women are permitted to lengthen their garments by one or two hand spans to cover the feet, or as a precaution against anything being uncovered by the wind, etc., but they are not permitted to do more than that, as is done with some wedding dresses which may have a train several meters long, which has to be carried behind the bride.

---

[118] Aḥmad, 6/254; see also *Ṣaḥeeḥ al-Jāmi'*, hadith no. 5571.

[119] Bukhāri, hadith no. 3465, *al-Baghā* edition - this is because he is combining two sins in one action.

[120] Abu Dāwood, 4/353; see also *Ṣaḥeeḥ al-Jāmi'*, hadith no. 2770.

51. Men wearing gold in any shape or form

Abu Moosa al-Ash‘ari (رضي الله عنه) reported that the Prophet (ﷺ) said:

> "Silk and gold have been permitted for the females of my *ummah*, and have been forbidden for the males."[121]

The market nowadays is filled with many numbers of items designed for men, such as watches, spectacles, buttons, pens, chains and so-called "medallions," made of gold of various standards, or completely gold-plated. One of the common sins occurs in competitions where among the prizes are men's gold watches.

Ibn ‘Abbās (رضي الله عنه) reported that the Messenger of Allah (ﷺ) saw a man wearing a gold ring; he took it and threw it aside, saying,

> "Would any of you take a burning ember from Hell and hold it in his hand?" After the Prophet had gone away, someone suggested to the man: "Why don't you take your ring and benefit from it (sell it)?" He said, "No, by Allah, I will never take it back when the Messenger of Allah has thrown it aside."[122]

---

[121] Aḥmad, 4/393; see also *Ṣaḥeeḥ al-Jāmi‘*, hadith no. 207.

[122] Muslim, 3/1655.

52. Women wearing short, tight or see-through clothes

One of the ways in which our enemies are attacking us in modern times is by means of fashions, which they design and promote, and which have become popular among Muslims. These fashions do not cover anything, because they are so short, transparent or tight; many of them are inappropriate for wearing even in front of other women or one's *maḥrams*! The Prophet (ﷺ) told us that these kinds of clothes would appear among the women of the last times — world approaching dooms, as reported in the hadith narrated by Abu Hurayrah (رضي الله عنه):

> "There are two types of the people of Hell that I have not seen: people who have whips like the tails of cattle, with which they strike other people; and women who are dressed but naked, walking with an enticing gait, with their hair looking like the humps of camels, leaning sideways. They will not enter Paradise or even smell its fragrance, although its fragrance can be detected from such-and-such a distance."[123]

Also included in this type of clothes are the garments worn by some women, which have long slits from the hem, or pieces cut out here and there; when the wearer sits down, her *'awrah* (i.e., all body except face and hands) becomes visible, apart from the fact that by wearing such clothes a woman is resembling the *kuffār* and following their fashions and trends of revealing clothes. We ask Allah (سبحانه وتعالى) to keep us safe from all that. Another serious matter as

---

[123] Muslim, 3/1680.

regards clothing is the bad pictures which appear on some clothes, such as pictures of singers and rock groups, bottles of wine etc., pictures of animate beings which are forbidden in Islam, crosses, logos of immoral clubs and societies, or bad words which do not befit people of honour, which may be written in foreign languages.

53. Wearing wigs and hairpieces

Asmā' bint Abu Bakr (رضي الله عنها) said:

> "A woman came to the Prophet and said, 'O' Messenger of Allah! I have a daughter who is going to be married; she had a fever and lost much of her hair — can I attach false hair to her head?' He said: 'Allah has cursed the one who attaches false hair and the one who asks for it.' "[124]

Jābir ibn 'Abdullah said:

> "The Prophet reprimanded that no woman should add anything to her head (in the form of artificial hair)."[125]

Examples of this include the things known nowadays as wigs and hair extensions, and the many evil things with which salons are crowded. Also included are the artificial wigs worn by some actors and actresses who have no morals.

---

[124] Muslim, 3/1676.

[125] Ibid, 3/1679.

54. Men resembling women and women resembling men, in dress, speech and appearance

Part of the *fiṭrah* (natural inclinations of mankind which conform to religion) is that men should preserve the masculinity which Allah has created in them, and women should preserve the femininity which Allah has created in them. Without this, decent human life becomes impossible. Men's resemblance to women and vice versa is something which goes against man's innate nature (*fiṭrah*) and opens the door to corruption and widespread promiscuity. The ruling in *Sharee'ah* is that when it is stated that the person who does a thing is cursed, that thing is *ḥarām*. Ibn 'Abbās (رضي الله عنه) reported that the Messenger of Allah (ﷺ) said:

> "Allah has cursed the men who make themselves look like women and the women who make themselves look like men."[126]

Ibn 'Abbās (may Allah be pleased with him and his father), also reported that the Messenger of Allah (ﷺ) said:

> "Allah has cursed effeminate men and masculine women."[127]

The resemblance may be in the way they move, walk and speak.

Similarly, the two sexes are not permitted to resemble each other in dress or by wearing anything that is specifically for the other sex. So, a man is not permitted to wear necklaces, bracelets, anklets or earrings, etc., as is widespread among hippies and the

---

[126] Bukhāri; see *Fatḥ al-Bāri*, 10/332.

[127] Bukhāri, 10/333.

like. Women are not permitted to wear things that are specifically for men, like the *thawb* (long garment worn by men in Arab countries), *shirts*, etc.; whatever she wears should be different in style, details and colour. The evidence that the two sexes should not resemble each other in dress is found in the hadith narrated by Abu Hurayrah (رضي الله عنه):

> "Allah has cursed the man who wears women's clothes and the woman who wears men's clothes."[128]

55. Dyeing one's hair black

The correct opinion is that it is *ḥarām* to do this, because of the warning mentioned in the hadith:

> "At the end of time there will be people who will dye their hair black like the crops of pigeons; they will never smell the fragrance of Paradise."[129]

This practice is widespread among those who have gray hairs, which they cover with black dye; this leads to many evils, such as deceit, and cheating people by boasting of something which is not true. It is true that the Prophet (ﷺ) used to dye his gray hairs with henna, which gave a yellowish, reddish or brownish hue. When Abu Qaḥāfah, whose hair and beard were as white as *thughāmah* (a plant with intensely-white leaves and flowers) was brought to the Prophet (ﷺ) on the day of the Conquest of Makkah, the Prophet (ﷺ) said:

---

[128] Abu Dāwood, 4/355; see also *Ṣaḥeeḥ al-Jāmi'*, hadith no. 5071.

[129] Ibid, 4/419; see also *Ṣaḥeeḥ al-Jāmi'*, hadith no. 8153.

"Change this with something, but avoid black."[130]

The correct view is that women are like men in this regard, they are not permitted to dye black any hair that is not black.

56. Having pictures of animate beings on clothing, walls or paper, etc.

'Abdullah ibn Mas'ood (رضي الله عنه) reported that the Prophet (ﷺ) said:

> "The people who will be most severely punished by Allah on the Day of Resurrection are the picture-makers."[131]

Abu Hurayrah (رضي الله عنه) reported that the Prophet (ﷺ) said:

> "Allah says: 'Who does more wrong than the one who trics to create something like My creation; let him create a grain of wheat or an ear of corn...' "[132]

Ibn 'Abbās (رضي الله عنه) said:

> "Every picture-maker (painter) will be in the Fire, and for each picture that he made he will be given a soul, and he will be punished in Hell."

Ibn 'Abbās also said:

> "If you must make pictures, draw trees and things that do not possess a soul."[133]

---

[130] Muslim, 3/1663.

[131] Bukhāri, see *Fatḥ al-Bāri*, 10/382.

[132] Ibid, see *Fatḥ al-Bāri*, 10/385.

[133] Muslim, 3/1671.

These hadiths clearly indicate that it is *ḥarām* to make images of animate beings, whether they are humans or different kinds of animals, whether the images are of two or three dimensions. Pictures are forbidden whether they are drawn, engraved, carved, etched or cast from moulds. The hadith which forbids making pictures covers all these methods.

The Muslim should accept what the *Sharee'ah* says, without arguing. Some may say "Well, I am not worshipping these pictures or prostrating to them!" But if you look closely and think about just one of the bad effects of the widespread presence of pictures in our times, you will understand the wisdom behind this prohibition: this bad effect is the provocation of sexual desire which leads to immorality.

The Muslim should not keep any pictures of animate beings in his house, because this prevents the angels from entering it. The Prophet (ﷺ) said:

> "The angels do not enter a house where there is a dog or pictures."[134]

In many houses, there are even statues, some of which represent the gods of the *kuffār*, which are kept for decoration. These are more *ḥarām* than other kinds, just as hung-up pictures are worse than those which are not hung up. How often have pictures led to glorification and grief, and led to boasting! We should not say that the pictures are kept for memories, for true memories of dear relatives and fellow-Muslims lie in the heart, and one remembers them by praying for forgiveness and mercy for them. One should remove all these pictures, or blot them out,

---

[134] Bukhāri, see *Fatḥ al-Bāri*, 10/380.

except when it is too difficult to do so, as with these pictures which are all over food packaging, or in encyclopaedias and reference books; even then, you should try to remove it, and to be careful about the bad pictures in some books. It is permissible to keep some necessary pictures, such as those on identity cards and licenses, or pictures which are walked on (such as pictures on carpets).

﴿فَٱتَّقُوا۟ ٱللَّهَ مَا ٱسْتَطَعْتُمْ ... ﴿١٦﴾﴾ (سورة التّغابُن: ١٦)

﴾So [keep your duty to Allah and] fear Allah as much as you can;...﴿ *(Qur'an 64: 16)*

57. Lying about one's dreams

Some people deliberately fabricate dreams and visions that they have not really seen, as a means of gaining spiritual prestige and fame, or for some material gains, or to scare their enemies, and the like. Many of the common people have strong beliefs in dreams and are easily deceived by such lies. The Prophet (ﷺ) issued a stern warning to whoever does such a thing:

> "One of the worst types of lie is for a man to claim to belong to someone other than his real father, or to claim to have seen something which he did not see, or to attribute to the Messenger of Allah words that he did not say."[135]

---

[135] Bukhāri, see *Fatḥ al-Bāri*, 6/540.

The Prophet (ﷺ) also said:

> "Whoever claims to have seen a dream which he did not see will be ordered to tie two grains together, and he will never be able to do it..."[136]

Tying two grains together is impossible, so the punishment will fit the crime.

58. Sitting or walking on graves, or answering the call of nature in a graveyard

Abu Hurayrah (رضي الله عنه) reported that the Prophet (ﷺ) said:

> "If any of you were to sit on a live coal and let it burn his clothes until it reached his skin, it would be better for him than sitting on a grave."[137]

As for stepping on graves, many people do this, and when a person is buried you can see people, who do not care where they walk (even wearing shoes sometimes), stepping on neighbouring graves, with no respect for the dead. The seriousness of this matter is clear from the words of the Prophet (ﷺ):

> "If I were to walk on coals or on a sword, or to mend my shoe with my own foot, it would be better for me than walking on the grave of a Muslim."[138]

So, what about those who take over the site of a graveyard and build businesses or homes there? As for responding to the call

---

[136] Ibid, 12/427.

[137] Muslim, 2/667.

[138] Ibn Mājah, 1/499; see also *Ṣaḥeeḥ al-Jāmi'*, hadith no. 5038)\.

of nature in a graveyard, this is something done by people who have no morals at all. When they feel the need, they jump over the wall of the graveyard and offend the dead with their unpleasant odours and impure waste matter. The Prophet (ﷺ) said:

> "I wouldn't care if it were in the middle of the graveyard or in the middle of the marketplace."[139]

Hence, answering the call of nature in a graveyard is like uncovering one's *'awrah* and answering the call of nature in front of people in a marketplace. Those who deliberately throw their trash into graveyards (especially those which are abandoned and whose walls are broken down) are included in this condemnation. Among the etiquette required of those who visit graveyards is taking off their shoes when they want to walk between graves.

59. Not cleaning oneself properly after passing water

One of the beauties of Islam is that it teaches everything that will improve and reform mankind, including how to remove impurities by cleaning oneself properly after urinating or defecating. But some people are very careless about this matter, and allow their clothes and bodies to become contaminated, thus causing their prayers to be invalidated. The Prophet (ﷺ) told us that this is one of the causes for the punishment in the grave. Ibn 'Abbās (رضي الله عنه) said: "The Prophet passed by one of the gardens of Madeenah, and heard the sound of two men being punished in their graves. The Prophet said:

---

[139] Op.cit.

'They are being punished, but they are not being punished for any major sin. One of them used not to clean himself properly after urinating, and the other used to spread malicious gossip.' "[140]

Indeed, the Prophet (ﷺ) said that,

"Most of the punishment of the grave will be because of urine."[141]

Not cleaning oneself properly after urinating also includes undue haste in completing the action, or deliberately urinating in a position or place where the urine can come back on oneself, or failing to clean oneself afterwards, or not cleaning oneself properly. Modern imitation of the *kuffār* has reached such an extent that some rest rooms for men contain wall-mounted urinals which are open to view, so a person who uses them is urinating in full view of anyone who comes and goes with no shame, in the midst of impurity. Thus he combines two abhorrent and forbidden acts in one deed; not hiding his private parts from the view of others, and not cleaning himself properly after urinating.

60. Eavesdropping on people who do not want to be heard

Allah (سبحانه وتعالى) says:

﴿... وَلَا تَجَسَّسُوا۟ وَلَا يَغْتَب بَّعْضُكُم بَعْضًا ... ١٢﴾

(سورة الحجرات: ١٢)

---

[140] Bukhāri; see *Fatḥ al-Bāri*, 1/317.

[141] Aḥmad, 2/326; see also *Ṣaḥeeḥ al-Jāmi'*, hadith no. 1213.

﴾... And spy not, neither backbite one another...﴿
(Qur'an 49: 12)

Ibn 'Abbās (رضي الله عنه) reported that the Prophet (ﷺ) said:

"Whoever listens to people's conversations without their permission will have molten lead poured into his ears on the Day of Resurrection..."[142]

If this person then goes and tells others of the conversation he overheard in order to cause trouble for them, then his sin of spying is compounded by another sin, as the Prophet (ﷺ) said:

"The eavesdropper will not enter Paradise."[143]

61. Being a bad neighbour

Allah has enjoined kind treatment of neighbours in the Qur'an:

﴿۞ وَٱعْبُدُوا۟ ٱللَّهَ وَلَا تُشْرِكُوا۟ بِهِۦ شَيْـًٔا ۖ وَبِٱلْوَٰلِدَيْنِ إِحْسَـٰنًا وَبِذِى ٱلْقُرْبَىٰ وَٱلْيَتَـٰمَىٰ وَٱلْمَسَـٰكِينِ وَٱلْجَارِ ذِى ٱلْقُرْبَىٰ وَٱلْجَارِ ٱلْجُنُبِ وَٱلصَّاحِبِ بِٱلْجَنۢبِ وَٱبْنِ ٱلسَّبِيلِ وَمَا مَلَكَتْ أَيْمَـٰنُكُمْ ۗ إِنَّ ٱللَّهَ لَا يُحِبُّ مَن كَانَ مُخْتَالًا فَخُورًا ٣٦﴾

(سورة النِّسَاء: ٣٦)

﴾Worship Allah and associate nothing with Him, and to parents do good, and to relatives, orphans, the needy, the near neighbour, the neighbour farther away, the companion at your side, the traveller, and

---

[142] Aṭ-Ṭabārni in *al-Kabeer*, 11/248-249; see also *Ṣaḥeeḥ al-Jāmi'*, hadith no. 6004.

[143] Bukhāri, see *Fatḥ al-Bāri*, 10/472.

those whom your right hands possess. Indeed, Allah does not like those who are self-deluding and boastful.⟩   *(Qur'an 4: 36)*

Harming a neighbour is *harām* because of the greatness of his rights. Abu Shurayḥ ( ) reported that the Prophet ( ) said:

> "By Allah, he does not believe, by Allah, he does not believe, by Allah, he does not believe." He was asked, "Who, O' Messenger of Allah?" He said: "The one from whose harm his neighbour is not safe."[144]

The Prophet ( ) regarded the praise or criticism of a neighbour as a measure of a person's goodness or badness. Ibn Masʿood ( ) reported that a man said to the Prophet ( ): "O' Messenger of Allah! How may I know if I am doing well or not?" The Prophet ( ) said:

> "If you hear your neighbour say that you are good, then you are doing well, and if you hear him saying that you are bad, then you are not doing well."[145]

Harming a neighbour may take many forms, including not allowing him to fix a piece of wood to a shared wall or fence; expanding one's dwelling in such a way as to deprive him of sun or air without his permission; opening windows overlooking his house and looking out of them to invade his privacy; disturbing him with loud sounds such as hammering or shouting, especially when he is asleep or resting; or throwing trash in front of his door.

---

[144] Bukhāri, see *Fatḥ al-Bāri*, 10/443.

[145] Aḥmad, 1/402, see also *Ṣaḥeeḥ al-Jāmi'*, hadith no. 623.

The sin of such deeds is increased when they are done to a neighbour, as the Prophet (ﷺ) said:

> "If a man were to commit adultery with ten women, it would be better for him than committing adultery with the wife of his neighbour, and if a man were to steal from ten houses, it would be better for him than stealing from the house of his neighbour."[146]

Some treacherous people take advantage of a neighbour's absence during his night shift to enter his house and commit immoral acts. Woe to them of the punishment of a painful Day!

62. Writing a will for the purpose of harming one of the heirs

One of the basic principles of *Sharee'ah* is that there should be neither harming nor reciprocating harm. One example of this harm is writing a will that deprives one or some of the legitimate heirs of his or their rights. Such a person is warned by the Prophet (ﷺ):

> "Whoever harms (others), Allah will harm him, and whoever makes things difficult for others, Allah will make things difficult for him."[147]

One of the ways in which a person's will can harm others is denying an heir his rights, giving an heir more than he is entitled to in *Sharee'ah* or by bequeathing more than a third to any one person.

---

[146] Bukhāri, *al-Adab al-Mufrad*, hadith no. 103; see also *Silsilat al-aḥādeeth aṣ-Ṣaheeḥah*, hadith no. 65.

[147] Aḥmad, 3/453; see also *Ṣaḥeeḥ al-Jāmi'*, hadith no. 6348.

In places where people are not subject to the rule of *Sharee'ah*, it may be difficult for a person to take what is his by rights granted by Allah (ﷻ), because courts that apply man-made laws may order that the unfair will registered with a lawyer be executed.

﴿... فَوَيْلٌ لَّهُم مِّمَّا كَتَبَتْ أَيْدِيهِمْ وَوَيْلٌ لَّهُم مِّمَّا يَكْسِبُونَ ﴿٧٩﴾﴾ (سورة البَقَرَة: ٧٩)

﴿...Woe to them for what their hands have written and woe to them for that they earn thereby.﴾

(Qur'an 2: 79)

63. Playing dice

Many popular games involve elements that are *ḥarām*; among them are games in which pieces are moved according to the throw of a dice, such as backgammon, etc. The Prophet (ﷺ) warned that the dice open the door to gambling:

> "Whoever plays with dice, it is as if he dipped his finger in the flesh and blood of swine."[148]

Abu Moosā (رضي الله عنه) reported that the Prophet (ﷺ) said:

> "Whoever plays with dice has disobeyed Allah and His Messenger."[149]

---

[148] Muslim, 4/1770.

[149] Aḥmad, 4/394; see also *Ṣaḥeeḥ al-Jāmi'*, hadith no. 6505.

64. Cursing a believer or someone who does not deserve to be cursed

Many people do not control their tongues at times of anger, and are quick to curse people, animals, inanimate objects, days, hours, etc. They may even curse themselves and their children, or a husband may curse his wife and vice versa. This is a very serious matter. Abu Zayd Thābit ibn aḍ-Ḍaḥḥāk al-Anṣāri (رضي الله عنه) reported that the Prophet (ﷺ) said:

> "...whoever curses a believer, it is as if he killed him."[150]

Because cursing is more common among women, the Prophet (ﷺ) explained that this would be one of the reasons for them entering Hell, and that those who curse will not be intercessors on the Day of Resurrection. More serious than that is the fact that the curse will come back on the one who utters it, if he says it unfairly. In that case, he will have prayed against himself and excluded himself from the mercy of Allah (سبحانه وتعالى).

65. Wailing (at time of bereavement)

One of the *ḥarām* deeds that some women do is to raise their voices in screaming and eulogizing the dead, striking their faces, tearing their clothes, cutting or tearing out their hair, etc. All of this indicates that a person does not accept the decree of Allah (سبحانه وتعالى) and is not bearing disaster with fortitude and patience. The Prophet (ﷺ) cursed the one who does this. Abu Umāmah (رضي الله عنه) reported that:

---

[150] Bukhāri, see *Fatḥ al-Bāri*, 10/465.

"The Messenger of Allah cursed the woman who strikes her face, tears her clothes and cries out about woe and doom."[151]

'Abdullah ibn Mas'ood (رضي الله عنه) reported that the Prophet (ﷺ) said:

"He is not one of us who strikes his cheeks, tears his clothes and prays with the supplication of the *Jāhiliyyah*."[152]

The Prophet (ﷺ) said:

"If the woman who wails does not repent before her death, she will be raised on the Day of Resurrection wearing a shirt of tar and a garment of scabs."[153]

66. Striking or branding the face

Jābir (رضي الله عنه) said:

"The Messenger of Allah forbade striking or branding the face."[154]

As far as striking the face is concerned, many fathers and teachers do this as a way of punishing children, when they strike them in the face with their hand, and so on. Some people also do this to their servants, even though this is an insult to the face with which Allah (ﷻ) has honoured man. It may also cause the loss of some of the important senses, which are located in the face, leading to regret and possible demands for retribution.

---

[151] Ibn Mājah, 1/505; see also *Ṣaḥeeḥ al-Jāmi'*, hadith no. 5068.

[152] Bukhāri, see *Fatḥ al-Bāri*, 3/163.

[153] Muslim, hadith no. 934.

[154] Ibid, 3/1673.

Branding animals in the face is done to make a distinguishing mark so that each animal's owner may be known and the animal may be returned to him if it is lost. This is *ḥarām*, because it causes suffering and deformity. If people claim that this is their tribal custom and that a distinguishing mark is necessary, it should be made on some other part of the animal, not on the face.

67. Abandoning a Muslim brother for more than three days with no legitimate reason

This is one of the ways in which satan causes division among Muslims, and those who follow the footsteps of satan may forsake a Muslim brother for no legitimate reason, but because of a dispute over money or some trivial disagreement. This division may continue for a lifetime, with one swearing that he will never speak to the other and vowing never to set foot in his house, turning away if he sees him in the street and ignoring him if he happens to encounter him in a gathering, shaking hands with everyone else but him. This is a cause of weakness in the Muslim community; hence the ruling on it is decisive and the warning against it is stern. Abu Hurayrah (رضي الله عنه) reported that the Prophet (ﷺ) said:

> "It is not permitted for a Muslim to forsake his brother for more than three (days); whoever does this and dies, he will enter Hell."[155]

[155] Abu Dāwood, 5/215; see also *Ṣaḥeeḥ al-Jāmi'*, hadith no. 7635

Abu Khurāsh al-Aṣlami (رضي الله عنه) reported that the Prophet (ﷺ) said:

> "Whoever forsakes his bother for a year, it is as if he has shed his blood."[156]

It is bad enough that division among Muslims results in their being deprived of the forgiveness of Allah (سبحانه وتعالى), may He be glorified. Abu Hurayrah (رضي الله عنه) reported that the Prophet (ﷺ) said:

> "The deeds of the people are shown to Allah twice a week, on Mondays and Thursdays; He forgives all His believing slaves, except for the one between whom and his brother is enmity. He says, 'Leave these two until they reconcile.'"[157]

Whichever of the two parties repents to Allah (سبحانه وتعالى) must go back to his brother and greet him with *salām*; if he does this and the other person ignores him, then the former is free of blame and the responsibility falls upon the latter. Abu Ayyoob reported that the Prophet (ﷺ) said:

> "It is not permissible for a man to forsake his brother for more than three nights, each turning away if they meet. The better of the two is the one who is the first to greet the other with *salām*."[158]

There may be cases where there is a legitimate reason for forsaking a person, such as his not praying, or persisting in immorality. If forsaking him will benefit him by bringing him to his senses and making him see the error of his ways, then it is

---

[156] Bukhāri: *al-Adab al-Mufrad*, hadith no. 406; see also *Ṣaḥeeḥ al-Jāmi'*, hadith no. 6557.
[157] Muslim, 4/1988.
[158] Bukhāri, *Fatḥ al-Bāri*, 10/492.

obligatory to forsake him, but if it will only make him more stubborn and persistent in his sin, then it is not right to forsake him, because nothing is achieved by doing so. Forsaking him will only make matters worse, so the right thing to do is to continue treating him kindly, and advising and reminding him.

In conclusion, this is what Allah (ﷻ) has enabled me to write about the prohibitions that are widely ignored. This is a lengthy topic, and in order that readers may further benefit, another chapter is needed, in which a group of prohibitions mentioned in the Qur'an and *Sunnah* will be listed. This will appear as a separate work, *in shā' Allah*. I ask Allah, He be glorified and exalted, by His Most Supreme Names, to give us enough awareness and fear of Him to keep us away from sin, and enough devotion and obedience to Him to help us reach His Paradise, to forgive us for our sins and, by His grace, to make us content with what He has permitted and keep us away from what He has forbidden. May He accept our repentance and cleanse us from sin, for He is the All-Hearing, the One Who answers prayers. May the peace and blessings of Allah be upon the Unlettered Prophet, Muhammad, and upon all his family and Companions. All praise be to Allah, the Lord of the Worlds.

Symbols used in this book

(سبحانه وتعالى): *Subḥānahu wa Ta'āla* — The Exalted

(صلى الله عليه وسلم): *Ṣallā Allahu 'Alayhi wa Sallam* — Blessings and Peace be upon him

(عليه السلام): *'Alayhis-Salām* — May peace be upon him

(رضي الله عنه): *Raḍia Allahu 'Anhu* — May Allah be pleased with him

(رضي الله عنها): *Raḍia Allahu 'Anha* — May Allah be pleased with her

Glossary

Adhā	أذى	:	Harm, it is harmful for a husband to have sexual intercourse with his wife while she is having her menses.
Al-Anṣāb	الأنصاب	:	Stone altars sacrificed to idols, etc.
'Awrah	عورة	:	All body except the face and hands for women and from navel to knee for men
Al-Azlām	الأزلام	:	Shooting arrows for seeking luck or decision
Al-Baqee'	البقيع	:	Graveyard in Madeenah where Companions are buried
Al-Fāḥishah	الفاحِشة	:	Obscene, shameful, vulgar, a major sin
Al-Fāsiqoon	الفاسِقون	:	Sing. *Fāsiq*; Rebellious, disobedient to Allah, dissolute
Al-Faḥshā'	الفحشاء	:	Indecency
Al-Ḥerra	الحِرَّ	:	Liberalism with women
Al-Kabā'ir	الكبائر	:	Major sins
Al-Khabā'ith	الخبائث	:	All evil and unlawful things, deeds, beliefs, persons, foods
Al-Maytah	الميتة	:	The dead animals — cattle, beast not slaughtered Islamically
Al-Munkar	المُنكر	:	Evil deeds, evil
Al-Muṭaffifeen	المطفِفين	:	Those who give less in measure and weight (decrease the rights of others)

An-Nuṣub	النصُب	:	Stone altars
Ash-Shirk al-Akbar	الشِرك الأكبر	:	Major *Shirk* (associating partners to Allah)
Aṭ-Ṭayyibāt	الطيبات	:	Sing. *Ṭayyib*; All good and lawful things, deeds, beliefs, persons, foods, etc.
Aṭ-Ṭiyarah	الطّيَرة	:	Observing birds for omens
Awliyā'	اولياء	:	Sing. *Wali*; Saints
Barzakh	برزخ	:	Phase between death and Resurrection
Bay'ah	بيعة	:	Pledge of allegiance
Bakhoor wa'ood	بخور وعُود	:	Types of burned incense
Da'wah	دعوة	:	Call to Islam
Daleel	دليل	:	Proof, evidence
Dhālimoon	ظالِمون	:	Sing. *Dhālim*; Oppressors, polytheists and wrongdoers
Fawāḥish	فواحِش	:	Shameful sins, illegal sexual intercourse; Sing. *Fāḥishah*
Fiṭrah	فطرة	:	Natural inclination of mankind, which conform to religion
Fuqahā'	فُقهاء	:	Sing. *Faqeeh*; Scholars of Islamic jurisprudence
Ghusl	غُسْل	:	Bath, ritual bath
Ḥallaf Maheen	حلّاف مهين	:	The one who swears much and is a liar or worthless
Ḥujjāj	حجّاج	:	Pilgrims; Sing *Ḥajj*
Ḥunafā' Lillah	حُنفاء لِلّه	:	Worshiping none but Allah
Ḥarām	حرام	:	Unlawful

Ḥareer	حرير	: Silk
Ḥasanāt	حسنات	: Good deeds
Ḥijāb	حِجاب	: Women's Islamic dress
Ilāh	إله	: god
Isbāl	إسبال	: Lengthening lower garments below the ankles
Izār	إزار	: Lower garment
Jāhiliyyah	جاهليه	: Ignorance, Pre-Islamic era
Janābah	جنابه	: Ritual impurity
Ji'ah	جِعه	: A kind of beer
Koobah	كوبه	: A kind of drum
Kuffār	كُفّار	: Sing. *Kāfir*; Disbelievers
Maḥram	محرم	: Somebody like father, son of husband, brother or father-in-law whom a woman cannot marry
Siḥr	سِحر	: Magic
Manāsik Ḥajj	مناسِك حج	: *Ḥajj* rituals
Al-Mashāhid	المشاهِد	: Sing. *Mashhad*; The Rituals of Pilgrimage to Shrines, shrines referring to graves or tombs of *awliyā'*
Miskeen	مِسكين	: Poor
'Ūd	عود	: Lute
Qāḍi	قاضي	: Judge
Qānoon	قانون	: Stringed musical instrument resembling a zither
Qameeṣ	قميص	: Shirt or upper garment

Rabāb	رباب	:	Stringed instrument resembling a fiddle (rebec)
Ribā	رِبا	:	Usury, interest
Rukoo'	رُكوع	:	Bowing in prayer
Ṣadaqah	صدقه	:	Charity
Sayyi'āt	سئيات	:	Bad deeds
Sayyid	سيّد	:	Master, leader, title for the progeny of Ḥasan and Ḥusayn, the grandsons of the Prophet.
Soorah	سوره	:	Chapter (of the Qur'an)
Sharee'ah	شريعه	:	Islamic Law
Shayāṭeen	شياطين	:	Sing. *Shayṭān*; Devils, Satans
Siwāk	سِواك	:	Natural toothbrush from the Arāk tree
Ṣalāh	صلاة / صلوٰة	:	Prayer
Ṣalāt al-Kusoof	صلاة الكُسوف	:	The eclipse prayer
Tabarruj	تبرُّج	:	Wanton display
Takbeerāt	تكبيرات	:	To say, *Allahu Akbar*, Allah is All-Great
Ṭanboor	طنبور	:	A long-necked stringed instrument
Thawb	ثوب	:	Long garment worn by men in Arab countries
Thughāmah	ثُغامة	:	A plant with intensely white leaves and flowers
Wali	ولي	:	Saint
Zāniyah	زانية	:	Adulteress
Zinā	زِنا	:	Fornication and adultery